Life Saving
Grace
in Jesus Name

(Manuscript, Poetry, Narrative)

Rhonda Jones

ISBN 978-1-68570-643-2 (paperback)
ISBN 978-1-68570-644-9 (digital)

Christian Faith Publishing
832 Park Avenue
Meadville, PA 16335
www.christianfaithpublishing.com

Printed in the United States of America

This very special version is dedicated to two beautiful children that suffered and sacrificed for their mother to have opportunities to become alive again.

My daughter Constance Jenel Jones was a constant resource when I became ill with a terrible disease of ovarian cancer. She spent hours in prayer as I went to treatments.

My son Joseph was a constant companion for wellness support and distant relations while attending a rigorous year of adjusting to a collegiate environment.

I also dedicate the book to an elderly mother, Emma Taliaferro, who, in her winter years, encouraged me to write with conviction and passion. She met her demise before the book was published.

I also want to thank my spiritual advisor, Pastor Arien Williams, for his encouragement and support.

The Lord has blessed our home again with health, prayer, and sanctification.

Contents

Prologue
Jesus's Name

This book of graciousness can be blessed with the attitude of transactions associated with the chaotic distance of readiness, resulting, at times, in a widely abusive road map. Please be cautious and reluctant to readdress the common reasons for doing unfortunate, caustic abusive lingo of longitudinal or reassess the current direction of reasonable, idealistic reputation of religion, roasting and revealing the readiness for discovery of circumstances associated with the guilt of consciousness.

The pleasant atmosphere is reduced to relatively a portion of private lives of associates. I kept reasoning the protection of lessons learned as a young woman that would not reject discovery warranted for gratitude. Remember, rest assured, assessment along life journey can't be marked with the distant trails of adulthood. The latter results can be considered rock bottom. Just as we are melting the clay of success to operate directly, the delight of heaven and satisfaction associated with the cloud of social injustices.

The racial divide is listless and unreasonable; the results are recluse, cowardly and cautiously; the coming-of-age is a reality for the rest of the world of sacrifice of the Windsor of random day results.

Chances Are You Were Right

But Jesus looked at them and said to them, "With men this is impossible, but with God all things are possible."

—Matthew 19:26

The Lord our Savior and Master will ultimately become our saving grace in a world of nonbelief—

The societal status quo is relentless in knowing why a person is not a saint in a time of trials but who doesn't have a living capacity of being satisfied in a life of nonbelievers—

The Christian value system that continue to be resourceful for more than 2.3 million adults in this country—

I hope one day the Lord will come to earth as a peasant and envision the works of the spirit—

Please be patient as he rises to the occasion of righteous reasoning of sanctified individuals—

The sabbath is restful and delightful for the reasoning of justifiable kindness associated with listening to a personal relationship with the Savior—

The depth of lifesaving grace is kinder than the living testament of Jonah and the whale—

The restless man can never find peace in a world not captured in a chance of living the last days and becoming overwhelmed in a day, concrete belief systems of chances, everlasting peace, and standard relationships—

Please forget about who said you could not or can't be successful in this life again, but remember the peace you have in knowing you can one day be a lady or man of candor and survival—

I once was lost but now found, blind but now I see—

The saints in heaven or earth are most likely restored during the second coming—

Please remember the last person who could not chance the store—

The reasoning behind not shopping at a place of comfort versus a place of solace is priority, prosperity, and legal sources associated with the moment—

I want to become isolated in uncomfortable environment—

The kindness of many sources is relentless chances to be a survivor—

The last thing the world should remember is that whatever things are joyful please review and consider these things—

The right place at the right time is really kind and restoring—

The joyful family guest list can be refusal to listen to the kind of accusations of resting—

Please send the kind of words of longing to fit in a peg of resentment—

The rest will one day come in fruition in the aftermath—

The graciousness of the Lord is getting ready for years of violence or repentance—

Please reference the wisdom of the Lord to be considered as the catalyst for coming to this playground of life and joyous occasion—

Please do not candor that could not be receptive at this point and time—

The loyalty of today is considered costly—

I do not want the person to be great inspiration to the people of a community towering for the less fortunate occasion of costly reputation of learning to be a part of a narrowing atmosphere—

The Lord or Savior considers listening into the regular situation—

I want the people or citizen to consider listening to a personal relationship with our Lord and Savior—

The relationship with family or friends can be revisited to the point of never coming together the greater the vain the worst relationship can get—

The reality of getting relief can be sent choosing the rest of your being a recluse in the land of the living and not getting the kind of response needed to address the issues of being kind, peaceful, lovely, relentless, and unknown—

The relationships of family and friends and the restoration of relationships—

The refusal of kind words can be resolved quietly and relentless—

The challenge of family and friends is not good personalities and resting in the century of restful choices associated with not being released—

The kindness of being released from the spirit realm into being not confident in a place of unbelief—

The solace of being uncomfortable or unkind can be relenting—

The home of personable being is not natural for a person to laugh at a personal not confident person is not being able to visit that personal atmosphere—

The lesson most people have is not seeing a personal longing for non-natural personal hang-up—

The lifeless personal response is never a giving rejecting personal livelihood of never being kind to anyone but yourself—

Ask your closest friend Who I am?

The response may surprise you as the personal response given by this individual called restless brilliance—

The kind of brilliance not seen by every kind of individual in this country—

Justifying the calmness of the soul can be wrenching—

The soul is the first place to be enlightened—

I want you to remember the Lord, God of host can't bless what you do not put into practice—

Please send the palace of heaven the blessings of Jesus—

Please be aware that the Lord of host can't bless what you want do for yourself—

Please put the offering in the tray, and the ham in the stove—

Please send the building fund money to the building—

Please praise God until all blessings flow—

Please send the check to the baker and utilities to the electric company—

Please awake children to the cross—

Please send the home of the cross is a receipt on vain or unreasonable glory—

The counsel of Jesus of Nazareth and the home of the cross is Jesus—
The lesson is peace the homage is learning the restitution of Canaan
and the cross was Israel—

Christ's Love Is Everlasting

Keep yourselves in the love of God, waiting for the mercy
of our Lord Jesus Christ that leads to eternal life.

—Jude 1:21

Reasonably the witness is a step in the right direction—
The saints forget who brought them to a kind renovation to a natural
    successful word of scenic religious purpose—
We are in a kind, reasonable, purposeful world of saints—
The witness of a place in time is a short memory of lessons learned—
The address of leadership is not valid of certain situations—
The resident purpose is challenging for an estate that was never
    invented for the purpose of living in an obvious reaction for the
    purpose of living—
Living in a world of obvious submission for not addressing a situa-
    tion dialect for the kind of lost caustic reform to the religious
    world to invent a generational relationship in a forceful world at
    the hands of the assailant for peaceful relations—
The educated wisdom for a timeless reaction for the justice friendly
    association with lasting atmosphere of descent rewards of char-
    acteristic reliance associated against realistic idealization—
The regret comes in many associated forms of adjacent revelation
    concerning the rest of societal realms—
We have seen Christian value systems turn toward the nonconven-
    tional in relevant years of societal history—
The changes we see are not from other traditional quality attire we
    are commonly used to—
People have decided conventional attire works much better—

The reference of the Christian is justifiable or determined to make changes according to the works of yesterday—

I continue to not understand nonconformity relations of different Christian religions of successful duty to the church's regular outfits of the twenty-first-century individuality—

Justice for the societal lesson the opportunity for reckless kind of moral language relaxing standards for the marketing relations committees—

Christ's love can claim the message of narrow roads for living in remorseful justice—

The Christian association with kindness can repair narrow escapes for normalcy—

Please choose life during a time of changing the course of living for Jesus—

The generations of attire reasonably can renew the lesson of returning to a natural state for the restful seasonal depth can be unconventional to the reader—

The relentless relating to the philosopher of the development of controlling listener—

I want the time to be located toward the educated adolescent or retention for the most irritated by the world attire for the future—

Lessons are taken for natural inquisitive addresses who can't control societal terminology for redemption—

Reasonably the irritated society can sense futuristic changes in a world for the merchant industry can result in natural authority—

Institutions are considering demanding a certain attire regardless of the changes in a systematic authority—

The Lord is rhetoric is changing in the delivery of the message for saving individuals for Christ—

The fraudulent saints have the lessons retrieved during the Sunday guidance—

The Lord is relevant in guiding me through during a time of jealousy for the lowest animal on earth his name is Lucifer better known as Satan—

He has trillion of people under cover acting as saints—

Situations often come to the plan for successful costly consequences, when individuals who violate God's plan for their lives are questionable to the least—

The Lord is a personal Savior for the lost will be persecuted for actions of persecution of the concrete solace of the greater environmental challenges—

The relationship for the next generation of the rescue for the client reaction to be secured for the greater good of societal confirmation and likeness for leaders who can't succeed in average situations of reality concentration of generalist throughout the lateral reversal of societal norms—

The Lord has leadership of the universe in latent control—

The kindness of reasonable persons for currently joyous relationship associated with certain counsel—

The selection process was negative consequences to the right at a normal—

Latent to the restless religious reasons that has never seen the righteous forsaken or begging bread—

The Lord has righteous descent for the restoration of the endless of others forsaken

Caustic justice for the relations of the world descending for the great commission—

Restless restitution along with a kind relentless treasure of gladness rescinding—

Advent can select the worldly creation for relationship building—

Thomas Edison created the light bulb associated to be settled around the rigid selective resources to be available to a world in vain—

Credible individuals often remember the unlikely presence of Jesus—

Extreme liberation is all the world needs in the event of a destructive carnage—

The reference is liberated in kindness of storage—

Shortages can rest pleasantly with the likely credible standards upon guidance—

Life guidance can one day be beautiful to the lively recent credible association of the glass genetic resources—

The location of the standards associated along wisdom of societal
   needs and climate of the world associations—
Shakespeare really required a dominant atmosphere reasonable sub-
   mission of deeds—
He once instructed a relative to be enlightened by sitting as a subject
   for associated references—
Societal concerns are controlled by subject concerns for the futuristic
   likely credible resourceful kind of exposure to living—
Christ will be a part of everything in life to guide associates with
   listening to atmospheric systems—
People resist the systematic cousins of the Christian sector for selec-
   tion processes determined by our Savior who let us be effortless
   in this life—
Christians should be available to other Christian believers as a
   resource—
Elders in the church are selected according to the life they lived for
   Christ—
Elders should be upright citizens in the church as well as in their
   homes—
Women should be Christlike along with their value systems that is
   relevant to keep values—

My Canvas

Be anxious for nothing, but in everything by
prayer and supplication, with thanksgiving, let
your request be made known to God.

—Philippians 4:6

Easiness is not a kind response to anxiety—

Anxiety is always associated with a person who dream dreams that
actually come true—

The truth of the matter is that kindness is associated with being a
person of character and resentment associated with dreams—

The carpet always wears right on the middle where all the traffic
walks—

Please realize that the road most traveled is really not necessary the
right road for you and everyone else—

White skirts, black pants, and pajamas do not make you a quality
individual—

These are not symbols that you have made it and a successful part of
society—

Society has more in-depth science of who it accepts into the class
of hall of fame. The class is a diabolical significant group that
appears and is not necessarily put together or made by any cer-
tain entity. The entity is often sought out by higher ups who
do not qualify for the class of elites, who work from skill and
circumstances find one another by accident while performing
everyday activities—

Rest assured the style needed to spend time equipping yourself for
the right group of people is sought after when you can happen

naturally from your weakness or your families' profession and invitations void naturally come and be a part of the picture—
The glass is always full-looking from the outside—
The inside is not necessary as bright or prominent as we are often dreaming of—
Remember who you are as a person and forget about whom you are seeking out—
Maybe the person you are is watching time and your glass is pretty full—
Please do not disappoint them—

Change

There is a time for everything, and a season
for every activity under the heavens.

—Ecclesiastes 3:1

When you are least thinking about what is about to occur some
changes begin to diminish who we really are or about to
become—

My first glimpse regarding change was the aging process continues to
emulate who I am becoming—

The graciousness of the people around me lets me know that I can-
not possibly understand what life is and what it brings to us—

The graciousness of the people around me lets me know that I can-
not possibly understand what life is and what it brings to us—

The challenge is can we be blessed with the graciousness of our Savior
and not accept who we are becoming on a daily basis—

Jesus sent his son to die on the cross for our sins and to be a healing
pool for all our shortcomings

Please agree that people are not certain what change has occurred but
can feel the intuition of change before we have consciousness
of change—

The cast for change may look different to anyone who could not
possibly believe the constant reality for perseverance—

I can't position myself for practices that are unique and creative for
the conscious satisfying comforter—

Releasing the avenue for change is the difficult partition for change—

When change comes so rapidly that you missed the change—

We can definitely resist the remainder of the time to sincerely respect what hasn't happened due to your eternal resistance to allow change to occur quickly—

Utterances of Satan

Resist the devil and he will flee from you.

—James 4:7

Satan attractiveness can be unreasonable but relentless to the person going into battle without the armor guard

The truth about the kind of resources Satan uses to trap his people from their sinless schemes

The genre is not ever going to change the course of wisdom that only our Savior can give to the depressed individuals

The universe is at a stance in this uniquely salvageable age of the last event that practicing satanism will destroy the rest of God-given souls that are held captive after being cleansed by the events that happened previously

Relenting to the actions of a satanic mindset can reasonably be reckless

Demonic reason for the actions of his following

Relationships are earned through sacrifice and determination of interrelationships of the universe connections

Individually the likelihood of torment depends on individual's self-esteem

The leniency is on

Satan tries to demand attention and seeks disciples to continue his immorality

Ethnicity is no problem when it comes to satisfying his internal for insertion of individual that will allow his immoral satanic anthems

He will never enjoy the company of saved individuals

The truth about Satan is his whole body is evil
Our Savior is always the winner although the catastrophic events can
  be life-changing

Shepherd

And when the chief shepherd appears you will
receive the unfading crown of glory.

—1 Peter 5:4

I once was cast out of the river where holy men were residing and
waiting on the Lord to be the type of person to win men to our
revelation and contrition—

I want to one day become the person that God wants me to be in his
kingdom and on earth—

The situation is uncanny regarding disobedience and being an indi-
vidual of integrity, character, and our alliance as Christians—

We can't release a spiritual relationship without first dividing our
regular understanding and allowing the shepherd to be free to
become an integral part of our being—

Jesus Christ will and has to be a welcoming connoisseur or appetite
for the beholder in order for him to be guidance for our lives—

Heavenly Father

You therefore must be perfect because
your heavenly Father is perfect.

—Matthew 5:48

The depth of our Heavenly Father can never ever be denied from
coming to school or preventive counseling regarding feelings—
I need to express to everyone the excitement that I feel when I say,
"Father, I stretch my hands to thee!"
The Lord is desperately attempting to arrive at a place in our hearts
that can't be replaced—
Friends have special interest in our patterns of our legacy that we
build our life and relationships to desperately arrive in the
latency of the depths associated with a lifetime of genuine rivals
that can be irreparable in leading the fouls of desperate attain-
able justices along with the freelance of being adjacent to the
experience—
Far long gatherings can be a remarkable moment for the progress to
be successful and attainable—

Disobedience to Our Savior

On account of these wrath is coming.

—Colossians 3:6

The sunset is equally visible to the poor as well as the reasonable costly pursuance of being a restless unheard-of person of total being—

The consequences are equally important to the saving grace—

The reality of living with a warm unsettling spirit continues to bring solace and unintentional warmth that can't be explained by our written saving grace—

The likelihood of remnants being destructive begin in tomorrow's relationship with the kindness of all our needs in a world of cruelty, discontent, and ridicule.

The justification begins with the solemn attraction of the craziness associated with not seeking the right person seeking awkward unnecessary attraction for foolish unnecessary cognitive behavior associated with no brain attention toward unexplained goals that salvage concrete behavioral statistics can respond to liable willing equally salvageable means for costly unreliable friendships in this area of discontent or unwilling costly unwavering situations—

The random escape from destiny cannot be escaped away from refuges of trauma associated with body aches, loneliness, biostress, and family dysfunction—

The selfishness of guilt associated with disobedience can lead to destruction.

Creativity

So then each of us will give account of himself to God.

—Romans 14:12

The sound gladness of being creative is succeeding the sound classic
adventure associated with coming to a land of immorality—

The closet of distress is leaving a comfortable widespread design for
the life of being shot by the creative bug of content—

Being an author is really a time-consuming art that cannot be real-
ized by telling tales of Jesus, but sharing the world with some-
one you care about and needs rewarding—

Instances of uncomfortable scenes that could frighten or adopt
friends who relate to your ever-written word.

I am not a scoundrel who wants to be noticed for my craft, but an
artist who wants to comfort a dying world without destroying
the artist within me—

Take note of an unforeseen world who has done so much advocacy
for dying religious world with selfless confidence that can't be
denied or destroyed—

The stain of selfish miracles of the lost art of writing—

The promise of living in a land of quiet, sensible, rational destiny for
familiarity of not knowing what life could have been without
knowing the quality of the shipping one another day of writing
to another day of writing to another publisher without seeking
the advances of my work or transferring the timelessness shelf
of creativity that is displayed in my home with several books
that need to be written about Jesus Christ my personal Savior—

The Deviant

Therefore, my brothers, whom I love and long for, my joy
and crown, stand firm thus in the Lord, my beloved.

—Philippians 4:1

Pleasure-seeking people, who do not want the world to evolve into
splendor but the consequences, are a restless society with little
hope for the future—
I want the harmony of people who don't understand the restless
domain—
I can't understand the restless domain—
I can't understand why in the world would people not be interested
in our Savior Jesus Christ—
The anxiety that has been uncovered is restless and disloyal today's
society of deviant immoral human beings who do not care
about the soul of a man not knowing who they shall become—
Dealing with symptoms of a sick society of nontemporal, restless,
sick nonconformity individuals who want society to conform
to their nonconformity to morals and family value systems—
I personally like the society of moral creatures who strive for the love
of Jesus Christ—
The Deviant throw morals away to be trampled and to be self-pleas-
ing to their own immoral ways and nonequality value systems.
The value system can't ever escape now each family or extended fam-
ily is scheduled to make decisions regarding future endeavors
and who will come to the home of the person, who really likes
a personal relation with Jesus Christ.

Jesus Christ will always be the ultimate judge of character and decide
who will meet him in the air—

The Lord judges us according to our deeds and circumstances—
Why we should not judge one another but let the Lord be the ulti-
mate judge of character with individual circumstances—

The Lord and Master

God is our refuge and strength, a very
present help in time of trouble.

—Psalm 46:1

As I review the world and the common inquiry that surrounds us on
a daily basis—
I have seen greatness appear in different corners of the world—
The likeness of the gospel tells me that the Lord can be present in
every situation—
Judgment should never take place in our hearts—
The greatness of the universe is that the Lord made us in his likeness—
References to the general makeup of humankind be accessed in dif-
ferent places—
Kindness is in all of us, typically when the kind of love the Lord
shares with us—
Transparency is provided on certainty and commands that sharpen
our psyche—
Living in a life without the Master has to be devastating event—
Chosen few for the work is announced along with the mentioned
frozen lives of citizens or people who judge one another that
surrounds or strength is psychological at times—
The reggae of listening to uncommon, unrealistic rhetoric by others
slows the futility along with sustaining progress—
Believe in who you are, along
With the kindness within—

Artistry

He has made everything beautiful in its time.

—Ecclesiastes 3:11

The canvas that delights our hearts can be restful, compassionate,
and reasonable—

Tools that are often reduced to letters of quiet style and collective
refinement from the creator—

Justification and irritated minds can be forgetful jaundice—

Letters are the unknown workmanship from the still or restitution—

Taken with care and not done in time of unconstitutional costly
rental and sabotage workmanship—

Resting in artistry is costly by chance—

The Leverage associated with the quality and cost of meaningful rela-
tionships has readiness for tears that can't be retrieved by time—

Justification for delivering a quality reasonable chance is in the care
of the artist—

God's kingdom and restoration were basis for his crucifixion and our
sins—

Jesus spent much of his thirty-three years on earth processing a dying
world is coming to all of us—

Problems can cause the most specific results to be conditioned by the
well-being of the scene it was designed for—

Tears Tested

Those who sow in tears shall reap shouts of joy.

—Psalm 126:5

Believing in yourself can ravish the importance of becoming a man
or woman of integrity and certainty—

The souls of many of men have been tried through repeatedly heart-
felt circumstances of the endurer—

Tears only represent the trials associated with cause or catalyst for
survival—

Emotional being only gives you leadway to an angelic being—

Jesus Christ can never be uncaring and only provide the divide
between emotional health for present circumstances and your
current futuristic battles—

Please remember challenges only bring opportunity for resilience—

The expedient way you resolve battles or problems quickly—

Protects the emotional well-being of the prescriber—

The certainty associated with our Savior can be candid, inspirational,
and angelic—

Reality of sadness associated with those tears is refreshed, revived,
and can be unconditionally a gateway to an inspiring relation-
ship with our Savior—

Revelation through tears is creative to the beholder—

The amplified creativity through tears could not have happened,
without the trials associated with weeping—

The most unraveled part of the tear, or unwanted part of the teardrop,
which is symbolic of the revelation gained through them—

Assurance

And this is the confidence that we have toward him, that
if we ask anything according to his will he will hear us.

—1 John 5:14

The Lord is faithful and just to assure we are confident in all situations—
The situations are not always true but justified beyond anyone's belief
  or desire to be within assurance—
Assurance is not always available to everyone that needs it but can be
  seen in uncompromisable—
The readiness is relevant to our desire for success and confidence in
  any situation—
Assurance is anyone person's desire to be well dignified or made very
  successful—
I can't imagine the kind of struggle you had as a child to make adult
  decisions very quickly—
Pleasure and assurance are uncompromisable
Please never forget who became in this short life—
Isaiah 7 says or explains if we ever become who we want to be—
The necessary steps are beginning to reach those necessary excerpts
  of friendships—
Isolation is a discuss of who the world really wants us to be—
Relevance to be an empty nester is not retrospective to me as an artist
  advancing my own concrete craft of narrative poetry—
The Lord will always assist me in my craft that expresses mostly my
  inner thoughts about who he really is—
The necessity to tell my story about the Lord in lay terminology is
  uncompromising.

The Shepherd

The Lord is my shepherd I shall not want. He makes me lie
down in green pastures. He leads me by the still waters.

—Psalm 23:1–2

I once was cast out of the rivers—

Where holy men were residing and waiting on the Lord to be the
type of person to win men to revelation and contrition—

I want to one day become the kind of person that God wants me to
be in his kingdom and on this earth—

Please remember we can't be a selection of tragic events, but joy to
the people we come in contact with—

The reader of this memoir should note the possibility of a good shep-
herd learning its craft—

The craft is related to being supper enriched with doing the types of
things that cause people to unite with going through the ranks
of being consolidated and their craft be seen in every situation
as possible—

The clothing of someone is not the thing that makes them who they
are it is what is in their heart and soul that makes them unique—

The Lord can cast a spell on the weakest individual but yet make the
person the next King or Queen—

I have not been single long enough to know the type of love that God
wants for me in a King—

I hope that person will love me for who I am, not because I have
something the person can use for themselves, but because they
love my smile—

Who am I as a person, faith, religion, morale, values, being the person I am and not for what they can get out of me—
Some people say you only live once—
I am not sure if that is true of our lives after a tragic divorce—
Of course our mortal lives never let us forget the unphysical deaths we have before we die—
People can kill your soul and inside long before your physical death ever comes—
Justification we have is our individual progress toward a go we have not reached yet—
Believe in the impossible and the impossible will happen for you—
The Lord is my shepherd I shall not ever forget his goodness and mercy that shall always follow me—

Reassurance of Suffrage

But God shows his love for us in that while
we were sinners, Christ died for us.

—Romans 5:8

The reassurance that a lamb can beat is the restful recluse of chamber
suffrage

I can tell the feasible distance between life is not going to relieve
suffrage

The lessons of many African venues are not challenged by the rooted
lessons of humanity

Reasoning of lasting results can be opinionated

Continue to be lost records of palatable rest

Please remember the culture of the African resource realm

The likely reason for the deletion of resources can be threatening to
the reviewer

Chances can be constantly reckoning the reality of coming events
that will one day bring

consequences to not making the right genetic reliance for the
justification

The grace record of leaving behind valuable techniques to survival

The man-clave is to be an authoritarian individual that will not waver
for the future of the angry slave master of yesterday

The revenue to diagnose the retribution for the last warranted cul-
tural reason for this is just being deniably sinister individual
who will not accept the change that comes with being rescind-
ing the history of the freeman

Justifiably classic, restful, historical, unpleasant chances of living a
    life of leaving behind the individuality of coming to a kind,
    unconcerned nation for the locality of the lonely disciple, who
    went against the freedom for the negligence associated with san-
    ity and gaining lost focus for the righteous historymaker
Please take a stance for the world is not kind or wasteful
The journey has a painful historical reflection
The humanity of the slave is slavery
The goal of restoration can cancel the hurtful chances to be captured
Believing in rejection of the last interest of chastening the long-last-
    ing cultural resource
The lonesome ranger often does not please everyone
The African American system does not always allow for injustice or
    criticism
The lost ransom for the lesson can be the guilt of not giving the
    reasoning associated with the graceful unpleasant ranges of sys-
    tematic restful alliances
Component lasts for the lesson on the caustic effective causes of not
    knowing the reason for not sharing the reality of unconscious
    suspense
Pleasantry is not providing the restitution but lasting for the reckless
    manifold associated with not being suspicious identity
Torturous false lessons can only harm you culturally
Please seek the kind recluse of sharing the beauty and veracity of
    being socially incompetent
Lastly, but uncomfortable realist can't possibly be a successful ave-
    nue for the quest for challenges that are not being established
    for reasons not identified by the uneducated individual costly
    chances of unreliable statue
Just vast chaotic changes to cultural lessons learned during an indi-
    vidual's childish existence
Thankfully, regret is not according to the lesson but systematically
    changes as life moves forward
Justice is often not served within a group of unreliable persons
Readiness, has no common place for kindness

Loyalty as a family is all we have as we become lonely during periods of suffrage

Please take the rejoicing of the label

The distant reasons of the restitution

Please listen to the years of reward that never is transmitted

The kind thoughtless chances for the reasoning

Look for the justice of the African hero!

Locally or logically the thoughtless and unkind persons can't rejoice during periods of triumph

The regions at the latest courses of my life

The rejects often release a negative connotation for the last resin

Please allow the ranked resources for the vast majority

Kelvinite is not the stone of choice but the completion of listening to the drummer of the hidden kindler associated with the giant continent that can't be revered Lastly, the comma is given to the reckless recluse not provided

Justly, please rest assured that when the slave received his meal on the ship he did not warrant any cleanliness or napkin as revered in the common clause

Don't be alarmed when the revenue is not available to the reasonably kind freedoms I want to sentence the rehearsal for the unkind soldier

I want to listen to the drum of the negative drummer, but the hammer of variance

Young entrepreneurs, willingly restore the restful peace

Giant Seminoles are seen doing the marches of the gulf coast slave

Tuesday morning is significant quest for the kind of quality that the manual laborer is used to

I just want believe in the distant flight associated with the vast majority of commoner

Qwert, kindness is not the answer for the distance

Joyous releasing is not gaining resources, but restraining the legitimate cancer of the slave

Resting for the southern culture

Reckoning can't be diagnosed by the tears of slaves

Justice is narrowed as time chances become limited

Hosea, receives a ransom for the collapsed, injustice associated with
ownership
Honey is easily obtained through the consumption

The Long Haul Home

The heart of a man plans his way, but the Lord establishes his steps.

—Proverbs 16:9

Reasonably, the ranks of the daring run cannot be realized. Please be a parental guide for the upcoming summer school semester. The lonely unadulterated reason for my expulsion from the semester can't stop because of poor performance in the semester before. The likelihood of you becoming a scholar is slim to none.

The school officials tried for years to get my mom to just come to the school for a conference. She always had a significant excuse for her attendance. I would always beg and plead for solace, but she would never attend. Justification would come from all kinds of sources: "I had to work late." "My car wouldn't start so I just can't make it today."

I always was the one with no mother at school. I finally realized my mother just did not care about school as much as I did.

Gently coming home from the store one Sunday afternoon, I asked my mom, "How come you will not come to school with me and meet my teachers?"

She simply could not answer the question.

"I never liked school," she replied.

My parents did not make it a priority for me. I should have done better with my children, but I do not care. I am sorry, son, for the noncompliant behavior of myself and not caring more. I would like to envision you to finish high school.

Justification is not warranted for my behavior. I just want to apologize for my actions. Please forgive me and your dad for not being more attentive.

The future for you and your children is very bright because you will care enough to be attentive. The world will be yours for your children and their children.

Just remember I want the best for you and those kids.

The loyalty you have for your children will always be the natural part of your living. When you grow old, do not let time hinder you. You will, one day, grow beyond your years. I did not care about having children and did not want any. I thought I would not be able to take care of them properly, and I could not.

The future of your children will be much brighter because you did a good job.

The world is yours if you make it. I hope you do and come tell me about it.

Please do not forget who you are, and success will be yours.

The reasonable diagnosis is to let the revelation begin as promised. The Christ of that day was anointed to be blessed by the Cavanaugh of the captive consequences of that time.

Christianity

Therefore if anyone be in Christ, he is a new creation.
The old has passed away; behold the new has come.

—2 Corinthians 5:17

Survival depends none on wealth livelihood or self-servitude
The Christian creed is often not a part of daily responses associated
    with the conscious reminder of reason and complex senses not
    part of reality but doubtful reasons
Retribution of kind redundant sources is not restrained from likeness
    and kindness
Please retreat to hindsight for guidance and higher powers for the
    guidance you need

Nativity

And in the same region there were shepherds out in
the field, keeping watch over their flock by night.

—Luke 2:8

The light is the light of living. The restless person will never gain any
enlightenment for the time spent leaving the home of Jesus. The
world can't imagine the time associated with the living during
the time when the Savior was born. The thrust of heartache that
his parents felt about the immaculate conception. The Lord can
never be associated with the wealth of the of citizens coming to
view this lifetime experience for the citizens of Bethlehem.
The reason for this experience is a rarity and a captive experience.
Please remember the time and the countenance for the time and
place.
The guest came to bring gifts to the champion of the entire world.
The gifts are an example of the experience of a lifetime. Please do not
ever forget the time of fortunate experiences.
Always remember the less equal presentations by citizens from far
away who would provide you anything to be a part of this glo-
rious event.
Listen to the crowd of onlookers and friends. The living has to believe
in the eternal brimstone of life. The reasoning has to become a
lifetime of justice and nonconcern for the goodness of a family
misplaced by a single lifetime of generations associated with the
history of the world events.
We, as humans, will never forget the eternal life we all hope for. I
have witnessed so many one-time events as the conception of

Jesus Christ. The event is witnessed in BC during the times of Herod. The witnesses were also during the time of our Savior being born. The ancient times were considered holy ones. The lifestyle was very dated and uncivilized. The constitution was nonexistent or even considered. The famine was in existence, and the lifestyle was simple. The time period was one of great loyalties to kings. The loyalty for royalty was learned during the beginning stages of life. The people of this time period were limited to the common man. The atmosphere was domestic and raw. The head of households were always men, even younger if there was no father. Women with no men in their home were required to consult a neighbor, family friend, or rulers during that time.

Please remember nativity is the immaculate conception of Jesus Christ.

Joseph and Mary had the first and only child without having intercourse.

Likelihood of chances for eventful challenges has been negatively displayed during the ancient time of nativity. The premise was to have the eventful event documented for the world to always remember. The most noteworthy event was out.

Is There Still No Place like Home?

A song of ascents. Of David. Behold, how good and
pleasant it is when brothers dwell in unity!

—Psalm 133

Reasons for the enlightenment is not what we have, but what we
ultimately can be happy with

The home is here for the escape from world events and the eventful
relaxation of the spirit

Listless opportunity can refute the kind warmth of the atmosphere
seen in the lilac resting place

The moment I came into contact with the statement of the relative
understanding of region atmosphere

The reason for the selection is not one of nature but of temperature

Parenting often cuddles the selection process based on the kind of
person who will reside in the residence

Ceiling height is the reason for the opportunity to be an owner

The price is a reason for successful venue, along with the cordial reli-
ance. That cannot be simplified

The lightning strikes during the unrealistic light during the day

Useless kind weather is not always the distance of the reassurance for
the spring air to rescind from the constant living of the reason-
able weather during the restful time that I spend relaxing in my
residence

The joyous time is the lack of friendly visitors who come to visit me

The recently vast of visitors following my beautiful decorative decor
during the time of their visit

I want the peaceful chance to be a likely believer for the tasteless creation

The home is a place for the steward to relax and create an atmosphere of peaceful, graceful charm

The sunlight is the main reason for the locality

Breeze through the window is sometimes being sent to the living sentence

The loving place for relaxation being ceiling-free to advance the daily regime for today

The reason for repairs is redundant actions of activity

The last reason for not having proper seating is not knowledge of the number of friends sitting

Friendly conversations that are likely to be seen among the visitors of a beautiful compound can often have great memories

During the months of September, August, and October you can fathom the bird's traveling to their destination. Readiness can also provide a time to watch from a window the shadow of winter starting a latened ransom for squirrels and leaves on the roof

The landscape of a home is just another reminder of the lasting cordial dynamics of the home. Generally someone can convince the alarming sound of the doorbell to be steadily ringing to express the company who needs to come inside

The reason for the gladiator sound of cheerfulness associated with the willingness of family to come and play, have dinner, or sit and talk

The list of visitors is various family, friends, companions, and associates along with the radiance of being in a homelike atmosphere

The desolate person who decides that a home is designed to be a part of the twenty-first century is seeking technology befitting for the logical task associated with doing business and everyday tasks for technology to be a natural part of building a competent home

The logical process for the home environment is not destroying the principal revenue that resides within the property

Technology plays a major role in the home

June is the perfect time for planting flowers and buds for the upcoming spring gardening and flower beds

The primary reason for being a new outstanding family to encourage, relax, and become a part of the environment pleasantry

The family must learn to be professional when it comes to learning technology

Please be engaged in family planning along with the technical responsibility

Records of past habits of technical knowledge sometimes can renew the leadership of the household

The dynamics of listening to a person in their home are beyond candor

Leather

On his robe and on his thigh he has a name
written, King of Kings and Lord of Lords.

—Revelation 19:16

L—Love is what time calls a test
E—Envision the earth being silent
A—Always believe that our time is predestined
T—Tell the world what silent is
H—Hear the grind of the world
E—Even the stars are silent
R—Risking everything can be enchanting

Realm of Calmness

For God gave us a spirit not of fear but of power and self-control.

—2 Timothy 1:7

In the realm of calmness, readiness, willingness, and self-control, the
    beat of the heart is the most requirement, resting in the dawn
    of night.

The repeat of the solace and the dawn of the day are the reasons for
    recall—what a pleasure it has been to restore the local resident
    of clients, associated with the dream of the coastal restitution.
    I believe, the next time the ball is hit, the reasoning behind
    the enlightenment is resonance of coming home in a reward-
    ing atmospheric gesture of readiness in essence is the target of
    mostly daunting chauvinistic views.

I have seen a multitude of languages that have taken precedence over
    the leadership of men.

The cancerous strain on the American people will, one day, be in
    vain.

The bravery of the United Kingdom as a whole will consume the
    leaders of yesterday.

Blessings often lead to successful, constructive caution associated
    with individual loyalty.

Pleasantry assets can provoke the same relationships of living the life
    of a personal relative revenue for caustic resolutions to prob-
    lematic relatively comforting rejects of past timing for some
    inadequate person of the listless life of phenomenal resolutions,
    specifically designed for the upper crust to expose pleasant
    occurrences of today's millennial millions whom do the Lord

makes accessible to be the person you become of the years. Our classes are developed in our minds and headstrong belief system that we learned to be viable value systems to emulate in the twentieth century and beyond the twenty-first century of civil indignities common to men of all cultures and races.

Justification is rising vastly as the commoner can dream about a tumultuous refinement of the century in central ascetic actions.

Rustful distrust of loyalties is royal phrases of very kind above-average individuals who are blessed with the best occurrences to have encountered.

I for one was a martyr for an organization that did not appreciate attitudes of famous or infamous trademarks of remarkable candidates from superiors or supervising the wealth of optimism associated with quality individuals that created their sophisticated entity. The organization did not recognize its own relationships with superiors.

Reconciliation from the wealth it encountered was due to their superior historians' efforts. I want to lavish the loyalty and opportunity for greatness is often never mentioned to downplay an image of superior founders and their concepts or ideas.

Peasants continue to haunt you long after your demise. I did not come to this place without sacrifice for the lenient dynamics of a confused existence for many, many years.

Loyalties died with unfamous and monogamous relationships that failed due to what inferior person people felt I had become.

The Lord surrounded me to give his concept that would, one day, change a worldly caustic regime, without preexisting warnings of deprecation for future ailments, amusement, and restitution, along with familiarity rejection among men.

People are cruel if left to their own devices, with no remorse.

Please forgive a dying existence of former cruelty crimes.

The forgiving God associated with a dying world.

Tragic Resolutions

I can do all things through Christ who strengthens me.

—Philippians 4:13

Tragedy comes and returns to their former selves
The creation, jobless, exploring expectations of themselves
The life that you live is resilience of everyone
The relations of hostage situations are resourceful, fantastic, explor-
    able, stronger, sophisticated, reliable, stern, and convincing
The cabinet of success is to be rejected and confront feelings coming
    to the time of conception
The less random person always leave in time of foolish significance
Readiness is going to be shared as the Lord randomly understands
    leadership being supplement by the target
Reasoning for this less fortunate being the love the for second national
    being song is righteousness, and graceful
Wisdom is a soul for the young gesture of kindness
The restful kind of people sometime costly humans for less fortunate
    individuals
Winter continues to be seen as a time of solace and randomly seeking
    kindness of grace of living a life of restless kindness
I can't imagine the tragedy of giving someone life of restless kindness
I can't imagine the tragedy of giving someone a great time to deliver
    the wrong kind of miracles to listen to the school of retaining
    the joyous kind of association of joining the clarity of signing a
    journey of chance
Please join the justice of gaining the grant of coming to a long jour-
    ney of the visiting rest of reading a lesson of champion water

Going to the real reality on the restless determined kind of reasoning of calling the well-suited case generations of the readiness of kind determined journey determined by the loyalty of human disasters of caseless journey to the disobedient sinner is gaining a distance of kind resources of living in a world where justice is different to me

The life of the common man can't be relied on every moment like the beginning chanceful dying kind, rustic, reliable, personal, dynamic, and locally spinning during Daring the local authority and social dynamic single lasting powerful justifiable leak proof unnecessary disgusting illegal lasting references to enjoying the less fortunate individuals for long-standing atmosphere of safety and despair to stand in the restful gathering of justice untold for the decency of the reliable conscious of dying people, unreliable, selfish, unconcerned individuals who do not care for less likely treatment

We as elderly people should send understanding conscious, grateful citizen who don't care about searching around the later part of working is adorable Please consider the reasons for just being you—The Lord can take care

Daybreak

And when Paul had gone up and had broken bread
and eaten, he conversed with them a long while,
until daybreak, and so departed.

—Acts 20:7

The sun is shining in strange, significant, unreliable, distasteful, unwarranted places

The life of a martyr, was not kind to the conspicuousness, reality, and revelations of satanic means

Please refuse to accept restless, nonenergetic amounts of rehearsed excuses not given to just any soul

Please take this restitutional atmosphere that can't or allowed to be explained I wish for common, reliable reasons for exploration in areas that the victim refuses to discuss and recall or mentally refuses to reveal past abuse, out of unseen loyalty to family arises, which they refuse and Shade abuse with mental difficulty self-induced protected barrier

The Jesus I know will one day send his comfort. To the culprits of unseen crimes

Crimes in relation to humanity are deplorable, insidious, unconditional abuse of natural circumstances of age, knowledge, timing, and ridicule of saints who never experience these types of experiences and have not seen persons of such circumstances, but blame the blameless

The excelsior person is reluctant to discuss fame and does not acknowledge the wrongs done individually

People want to refute what was personally done

Please extend prominence of unrealistic persons of reluctance to the personal selfish will of reduction in relation to former classic friendships

Please come before a natural rejection not displayed by most humans for fear of not being rejected by mankind

The resource of charity depends on societal pressures

The restful nation of prudent leaders oftentimes has forgotten inaugural sophistication

The worldly phrases are changed richly as world progresses toward unfamiliar affairs of today

Governments attempt fabrication as an answer to being knowledgeable significance

Please resist a worldly chaotic moment of being unconstitutional reliance

Satanic Intuition

That the God of our Lord Jesus Christ, the Father
of glory, may give you a spirit of wisdom and
of revelation in the knowledge of him.

—Ephesians 1:17

Just seek biblical guidance when the world will not love the obvious
senses of God I can't fathom the world not understanding the
costly challenges of not understanding faith not able to recon-
struct the lively restful state of being in a battle with a selfish,
inadequate individual

The person doesn't realize the costly location for not wanting Jesus to
be a part of their lives

The esteemed maker of the land and sea doesn't acknowledge his
reverence for our lives

The wrong attitude is conditional to actions

We have done so much wrong the world has become comfortable
with doing illegal profiting actions from watching the storms
that place individuals in these situations

Jesus is a healer of these storms of restless concerns for the universe of
generational actions of others

Satan is a liar of many immoral actions of several unconditional
partnerships

He seeks to eliminate the person and his chances for successful future

Jesus says we can be excellent stewards of our lives and value the suc-
cess and challenges that come with being successful

Keeping from successful activities that break the knowledge barrier
for the many societal needs

Jesus will once again love the battle, but reasonably keep being the champion

The guidance can be one that no one can stop being a servant of the Lord

Resting is not an option for satanic individuals

The goal is justifiable in a mind of destruction

Satan is not relevant to the deeds of a dying system of individuals that believe in him

The attitude of the individuals is just not kind in a short reliance on citizens to assist with activities that harm people of faith who stand with the Lord

Their hearts have satanic activities on the inside of them that don't stop or rescind activities he plans for future latent, unreasonable, stupid judgment for the world continues to change rapidly under the direction of their satanic approach

Loyalty

Love bears all things, believes all things,
hopes all things, endures all things.

—1 Corinthians 13:7

The time has come for a place of loyalty toward humanity
Humanity can never be controlled by an individual or individuals
Just remember the time and place for future accounts of loyalty
The most important person is you as a role model in a world of discontent unhappiness
The logic is the more you achieve the more the world will surround you with becoming gainfully
secure and consolation, reality, and realistic choices that cannot be defined
Please consider your future and location for planning a life surrounded by loyal friendships, unhappy souls, kind friends, and satanic attacks
Please remember the people who cared during your hardest time, God steps in and reduces the pressure from the massacre
Please release, live, and do not ever give Satan a refuge of condemnation and disloyalty
Restless condemnation is relevant to the reasoning of fancy justifiable, relentless, terrified, fortunate, abundance and grace
The Lord has always been her crying hour of peace and reliance on the holy spirit

Kind Hearts

Be kind and compassionate to one another, forgiving
each other, just as in Christ forgave you.

—Ephesians 4:32

Devils do not always come in their original outfits, but come in street
attire

The moment that you know whose you are chances are slim for their
consideration of others emotional fortitude, gratitude, guaran-
teed loyalty, sophistication, satisfaction, faith, reality, and com-
mon ground

Please consider the heartaches of this life, confidence in self-suffi-
ciency, kindness, trust, religion, and your personal value system

It will take the rest of our lives to be transitioned to a place of kind-
ness, reality, faith, the will of the lead church

We must consider who we are as people of today

The hope we have for others to be just as successful

Please look for a natural way to express love, readiness, infamous
causes

Please consider each individual to be a latent of kindness, freshness

Please come to the conclusion of statements associated with a world
of destruction

I have never seen the expedition of kindness

The stressors associated with this life of deterioration are in question

We should provide guest with respect to the press by them on the
streets of his country

I am late for things that should have already happened

The justice of a world not yet seen is causing unnecessary painful memories

I want to forget the love shown to the unknown souls we are unsure about who will become

The lives of friends are never a competition of people we care for

The lives of people are contrary, pleasant at times, but narrow is the rudeness of others who do not care about the lives of others I want a season of friendships of restless restoration

The expectations are relentless or priceless to whom those individuals could disturb

I don't want unclassy incidents of relationships

The cousins of these happenings can't hurt anyone but the beholder

We do not have leadership to come to realize the successors of this contribution to the world

The world has stamina, guidance, religion, and rigorous contention

I just cannot forget former thoughts, associated with righteous perfection

I will not understand request performed under stress

I will not forgive this land for rigorous, insidious, constitutional reliance on the needy, for sufficient abuse

Specifically the race is often forgotten. In which condensation builds nonguidance

The level of the risk, is not lost or forgiven

I will one day master the life I once knew

I will steal days reduction of poverty and abuse

Please come to the conclusion of monetary reliance that may release restitution

I am praised for not providing a life given to others

Please gain reality confusion along with people not being forgiven

Please allow differences of causes that will have a candlelight resources of circumstance

I am in a relationship with a powerful instinct of characteristic circumstances

I will not blaspheme a past condition to encounter a relief physically

The culprits are waiting upon acceptance to a problematic world built according to their unbelief, knowledgeable, restful peace

Patience

The end of something is better than its
beginning. Patience is better than pride.

—Ecclesiastes 7:8

The lives of people are often released to the person of servitude

The home of a sane man is unreliable according to the resources in
the bible or biblically

The host elf is considered soundful and questions their choices

Be reliable to the people of the universe

The queen is always the person of utmost authority

I wish people would seek the loyalty of strange relations that com-
promise the realist transcript of hustling through the crises of
reliable persons

I have seen questionable situations of confusion and strife

The upsetting emotional abuse is hazardous to health of the
predecessor

Governments are rude, unsuccessful, foolish, unreliable, and
controlling

The heartache of pleasing someone is to begin a life of successful
relationships

The pleasure of compromise was once a derivative of hope, charac-
ter, persecution, heartache, stamina, resolution, giant persecu-
tion associated with world events and claim people for human
trafficking deadly affairs, imprisonment, and candid reality for
slave traffic I want the world to understand real soulmate rela-
tionships that are not always associated with the opposite sex or
orientation

The problem is reliance on the kindness and influence of others who do not understand the glory associated with cleaning the sources of people and the common reality associated with caring for people as a whole thought

Please be patient as the events associated with a God of peace, tranquility, abstinence, reality, customs, culture, creed, unanimous hope for kindness to others

Come to a place known as hope for kindness to others

Come to a place known as hope, chest of prominent wine, classic culture, realist, short anchors, storms, and cold ambitions

I have a winning resource that we as competent companions can never expose ourselves

The doors are endless, nontraditional, embalming, assassination realistic moments of fortitude, guidance, along with a winning personality with sons, classic repose, and dominance for mankind to be enjoyable to God's certain people

Self-loathing is constant reliance on the right people during the right things for joyous occasions

Do not criticize others for not being the exact same as you

The Crosses We Often Forget to Bear

And when he called the people unto him with
his disciples also, he said unto them,
Whosoever will come after me, let him deny himself,
and take up his cross, and follow me.

—Mark 8:34

At the cross, at the cross, where I first begin to envision life trials
The Savior had not yet come to me with supplication or dignity
The livelihood of the world is not a good place to be
The stronghold of witnesses to suffer against the refuge of the jungle
    not created by man
Please continue to allow Jesus to be a comforter in a land of empti-
    ness I do not want a fortitude of accomplishments just to reveal
    a life well lived
Please be comforted as you go through trials of the infidel
The infidel always joins the freeman to make things difficult and
    release a clean struggle
The struggle is divine and resolved through a crisis of the happy
    realist
Do not ask a question that is not acquainted with the realm of
    evidence
Please seek customs that do not matter for most of us in harmony

The Sweetest Name

O Lord, you have searched me and you know me.
You know when I sit and when I rise;
You perceive my thoughts from afar.
You discern my going out and my lying down;
you are familiar with all my ways,
Before a word is on my tongue You know it completely Oh Lord.

—Psalm 139:1–4

The game kept going, but the time was not a good self-portrait of the
life I used to live
The cards are rare within this night of safe beginnings
The safest places are sometimes the incomparable or compromising
grace and single most deadly places to be
The struggle is with the sun setting around the time Jesus was being
entered into compromising position
I oftentimes would not allow the realist in me to prevail
I want to be in a land not made by commonwealth
Please be desirable to everyone in this exposed entity they the world
Please stop the massacre that was once involved as the source of
familial society
I can't discuss the life provided to me in a world that no one knows
about
Please realize we can't be studied enough to leave this solution
unresolved
The sun is not a place to ever leave the saints' societal law compromised
I am disgusted at lives that will not accept such upstaging when
studied

The life of wealth confusion is unreliable

Please release the rescuers of entrapment

I do not want to ever envision myself in a state of confusion as I witnessed in this lifetime

It tears up a person who was once loved by so many people

Please provide an opportunity to discuss our lives with others who did not know what happened to them during a lifetime of poverty and witness turmoil massacre that they now can not exactly recall the days of old despair and inhuman tragedy

I want to always remember to be thankful for being in a mindset that has not met its demise before my earthly temple dissipates

Please consider the frontal lobe of every mindset that was made uniquely for each witness's mind deterioration in a person we once admired, depended on, preyed on and discovered that they can't relinquish past abstinence of the mind that could once understood the morning in the past and present frock

Please tell their life story as accurately as the enlightenment recalls events of harm in the precious name of our Savior

Servitude

Let all that you do be done in love.

—1 Corinthians 16:14

I do not like the world as it is right now

I have been attacked and still depend on the life of stalemates, who
are unkind to one another

Please be an anchor to a world that was once the home of the slave

Please never forgive the dominant behavior of the significant country

The home of the slave and slave master

I know one day we will stop and realize that God has anchor of ser-
vitude to him that we can't forget

I do not have the right mind of citizens that had to fight to vote in a
land that can never be free of servitude

I ranked as a person who did not come to live a life of realistic
challenges

The most important avenue is to give your entire being to the most
successful available person of the sincere reality, but we cannot
be given any authority without being totally unconditionally
motivated

We could resource our daily commentary without any person being
available to be successful

Please consider the consequences if being enlightened by a similar
entity of servitude

The presence of certainty of reliable persons can't succeed unless
strife is provided with the label of joy and less confusion

I want the world to lessen disciples who have a protective barrier

I can't fathom the deliverance of all kinds of revelation associated
with human from systematic review associated with the hostil-
ity of human disloyalty to devotion in the lasting world of ques-
tionable belief of the kind of revelation in the realistic venue of
happiness associated with humanity
The real problem belongs to a staff procedure of the justice of the
single massacre associated with everyday living
I want to limit the type of person to be a longtime friend and territo-
rial entity of truth and prosperity for generations of rapture and
exposure to the freeman who came to us from unknown places
to equip the man who never would have come to the rescue
man from places to be wept in a total massacre of shame, abuse,
loyal fortitude, acknowledgment, greatness, pleasurable news of
the loyalty of Christ's forgiveness
I wonder day, night, years, phantom lesions of kind remarkable pub-
lic display of leadership that can't be used without someone to
listen to
We begin lives with the breath of angels that angelic beings cannot
cause fortitude of hope literally listening to the wrongs of free-
man from long after the future man

Resting

Come to me all who are heavy laden and I will give you rest.

—Matthew 11:28

Realist says you can never ever say something that will let you see
the kind of person who just cannot cease the friendship of the
lesson to be in serious trouble

The character of the children would not have to be seen by then the
similar person is gone from the store

Rest assured the level of confidence is vastly critical

The key to learning the census of crying most of the time

Respect is relatively lost in the premise of the relationship with time

The victim is your source of kindness and loyalty to the grace and
love

The light of today is the volume of self-discipline which is a difficult
task

Reckoning the universe along joyous saying satanic meeting can cause
a raging sundown by dawning eye for the lively skating through
time and understanding the reluctance to have an inner strategy
for living through exact safety tool for living

The relations can't be reasoned with the cleaning of the sanity that
cannot be seen the loyalty of reward is not at the same person
in control of the word of searching until the light shines in poor
sanity can never be restored to its original state so do not forget
the slave in chains in America

She lost her sanity in the world, she wanted to live beyond her time
and be sane

The world did not accept her uppity ways of doing things

She was beaten and drowned for being who she was
She was taught by the white man to be so
The world was not ready for her smarts in that area
She would not give her, her learning up
At the end she knew she was not herself and tried to fit in
The world disliked her for it, but her mind told her just to survive
the massacre
She was not able to fight anymore and died trying to be something
she was not by people who wished they were half the woman
she was she could keep a tap on a shoe but had no education to
be the person she was in her mind
If anyone needed educating the world did
Clothing makes you some, but life did not allow such
There was a history of mania in the family, but she was hit in the
head also had the intelligence to reach and teach and her daugh-
ter had the gift but was hit by jealousy as a young child that
caused cowardice to continue some
Life can grow you to overcome obstacles, although the curse was
always beckoning in her history
The world saw the not coward child in school, but before she was
five years of age
Members of a refined black community always wanted to tell the
story but dare not tell the world she fought to overcome

Celestial Anthems

For the wages of sin is death, but the free gift of
God is eternal life in Christ Jesus our Lord.

—Romans 6:23

Please have heartless speech with the uncontrolled angel of the night
air

The leisure pleasure associated with this nondecisional ecstasy of
human nature I want to one day say to the lonely the restless
people of the entire human atmosphere I know one day the
leadership will come to a, where a no work left for someone to
complete I once had a sleigh that did not allow me to come to a
place of sanctuary alliances with our species, culturally, spiritu-
ally, socially, and cowardly

Please consider the inhuman atmosphere that is a part of our not
living lives that were once vibrant, successful, complete, and
wholesome

Selfish people keep taking care of themselves regardless of the home
being reduced to plummeting pettiness, insecurities of the reli-
able standards we once called family, friend

The deep understanding associated with the celestial being can never
be controlled

When the word has given up on you

As a person of successful leadership

I want the government of societal judgment to be prepared for celes-
tial being changing my life structure

Please seek counsel, not from everyone, but from freedom of societal
judgment I can't fathom being left behind the mainstream for-

tunate, prosperity associated with witnessing the anger, defeat, unhappiness, and slavery of the human being

Please persevere toward a mentionable celebrity stain removable to bring a common ordinary person into a creature not known at this very moment

The desirable stances of each and every human deficit is their struggle for humanity and kindness associated with judgment

Please continue to allow Christ to intercede in a way that can't be destroyed

The worst and most understandable person in this celestial world can't rely on judgment of others in this land of opportunity, successful intervention along with opportunity, successful intervention along with opportunity for trust

When the world has given up on you as a person of successful leadership I want the government of societal judgment to be prepared for a celestial being changing my life structure

Please seek counsel, not from everyone, but from freedom of societal judgment I can't fathom being left behind the mainstream fortunate, prosperity associated with witnessing the anger, defeat, unhappiness, and slavery of the human being

Reluctance to Survive

Therefore stay awake, for you do not know
on what day your Lord is coming.

—Matthew 24:42

The law of attraction is a sense of survival technique for the law of
  level outstanding
Chances are the level used by the cute girl is not warranted
Choosing not to stand, can restore a terrible relations with the stan-
  dard surprises to send to many composers who can't solve the
  problem with certain legacy and sense the belief of greater exis-
  tence for January along with the grand scoundrel of esteemed
  dirty raw class for the kind of united respect
Dance the life reviewing entire unique custody of strategy
Just in case the leniency of the world is destitute to survive
The longitudinal life of the person will continue to be available to
  the rest of the world
Having someone to be a valiant person of the universe
Just in case God did not come in time he will have the caustic person
  to lose faith for family and self
The realization of not having enough funding for simple things is not
  being dominated for reasons unknown to a stellar God without
  prayer for preexisting sails
The window of viable perplexity is not available for sensitivity
Available for the necessary reasons for fortune is not available to them
Righteousness cannot be seen or listened too by other, you have to
  take the owner's words and
acknowledgment

I am the right person for the present mindset of a dying world

The class of a person is not equal to their ability to diagnose the system as we know it

The pledge is to forget the diagnosis and get direct to the individual that caused the massacre I do not want my Father to be displeased with the culture of a system to make sure we did not answer the allegiance to the unknown government alliances

I can't understand such intolerable people who claim they do not understand the regular stance associated with the peace and calmness of alliances for future exploration

The personal agenda is not important to the race of a legislative process already in place and cannot be changed easily by the process or the leadership of standard reluctancy associated with the small episode discussed years ago to come into action on regular divide and reluctant savory distance

Please leave a legacy to explain the harshness of the people during this industrious unlikely physode

Dancing with innocent blameless eyes is too illegal to be seen by the people of ignorant circumstances

Excellence takes time to be exploded by the honorable senior citizens of that period

Lessons should be evidence of the familiar atmosphere of the legacy for the turning the clock back for the human mind to frequently understand the likely expedition for a jobless person with destiny limited to be abused according to authority at human dignity is destroyed for the listener to reap the benefits along with rewards

Stellar company along with appearance can solve many problems associated with custom religion gallery

The student with the most gratitude is welcomed to the kind of structure for the Lord can be a source for the generation revelation of the Winston

Destiny can receive the witness of changing your attitude for the raging spirit

Elizabeth is a welcoming spirit for the choices of common resolution

Justice is illuminating the spirit to justify the saint who turns into a
relative common secular resolution
Justify the class associated with their chance of creation
Rustic pillow is not beneficial random
The lesson to learn is to last for the lifetime of resources of the last
content
Just hear the counsel for religion destitute of common law existence I
want the common man to listen to the excerpts of the economy
Hear the tone for the common marching of a fellow citizen
Life is not just existence, it can be to just live according to the last
quiet person to express the lasting results of the rest of my
existence
The look of climbing to the element of surprise is not necessary the
reign of the journey of lasting the season is this a person to raise
a girl child
Just listen to the heart of this person
She doesn't know the subject matter to just listen to the universe
She began to just beat me immediately for just being in her presence
The person was an immediate enemy for the life of my existence
She continues to express harm for being a human that I have to take
care of
I did not like children in my presence
Listen to the whole expression of the scenic view before judging a
person of my candor
I love Maya Angelou's spirit and spiritual being
She did not judge others but simply taken advantage of opportunity
to believe in herself as an artist
Please consider the tactful experience of others who came before us
I am likely to be in likeness of the way we wear our hair and the atti-
tude of noncowardice
Living in a world of great discipline where laws prevent us from
becoming seen during the chapter to be seen in modes of
creativity
I want the Lord to forgive me for being me
The world allows you to have fun without the same consequences

Lessons are not always in the light of being stolen during the time of
restoration

I could not forgive myself for this act

Please take the time to forgive myself for the deeds of the walking as
a person of faith

Report the cowardice distance that I had having fun in the South

The Lord will provide a way for you and for me the guidance of
Kings and Queens

The Lord has not left you, we leave him

I do not know who is right and who is wrong in this life

I do know the Lord is available to me and to you

Rhonda have to believe we are a mortal of just being available to the
Master

Definitely, I stand and cannot call the murder of just being available
to the guide of listening to

the person on the tape of the power of gratitude and sincerity

I can't watch the dawn of the daybreak the noonday Sun

Please rest tonight under the noonday sun I can't listen to that kind
of talk because the counsel is a forgiven source of communica-
tion justice is identifiable

Do not forget who made the illumination of the Sun who has begun
to see the dawning of the familial relationship—the cowardice
presence

I believe you will one day see livelihood of Kings and Queens

The road is a difficult one but you can make it

Please remember who came to visit you and you will become the wise
person you think you are

Join the group of felon workers who thought things would never
happen

Life is a chance you have to endure for a short period of growth

The weakness is not the sense of the selfish man but the stupid unre-
liable person, who never forgets to send the world under siege

Be true to yourself and never forget who you are

The kindness shown to the confused person is not seen I will not
understand the trail of the Christian faith of the long limited
chance to make things less kind and if you cannot understand

the wisdom of the longtime friend of the trail associated with
the lost wisdom and love
Please try to stay on the trail to happiness and the guilt of having a
baby at my age
The child doesn't deserve to have old outdated parents to raise them
Just try to boost yourself up from day to day like all of us

Stiffness

Should not the multitude of words be answered?
And should a man full of talk be justified?

—Job 11:2

The rest of assurance is reading the cards
Please resist the attitudes that cannot restore the business of the questionable to the concentration for the being questioned
Justification associates with the business high goals
The release of the company of associates and atmosphere relations
Reading the likelihood of common fears
Can believe the new chances for survival
The left justification which became vast currently can be kind of seasonable meaning of the rights of people and the killer for the multitude of financial cremation
The culprits can now become listener to the Mafia justification
Chances of the dreams are less boredom for the living sacrifices of the financial stability
The monetary value human existence cannot be betrayed for the beating of the kind of the reasonable licensed registration of the genius
Rhonda has the rights of any other person in the class for disputing the release of negative persons
The loyalty of friendship for clothing and blood clotting and the knives of the monetary business zeal
We should be left with dignity along the quick wellness and the twentieth hour of loss reasons for the temptation of providing a system to be changed for the lives of living for the last children

who could not be along the side of the lasting dependent of resources in the inventions of the infidel of the believed person of cleaning of the last of the reticent allies of the south random secrets of the only goal of completing the citizens who participated in the employment

Culturally, the scripture is to release the kind of restoration and negative genius of the loss in the father who never sentenced the bracing of the girl who would become Satan's prey for immorality to come seeing the lasting change

Charles Luciano was in the most organized criminal based on one of the best-selling materials on organized crime

Decent, relations are difficult to change the reasons or restore individual dignity

The resident of language is often sent to the rescue of tomorrow's feelings

Reasonable resources for the gentle lasting consequences for their crime

Jesus can always sense the relationship for the lonely individual sources

The home of an indigent individual is always left for the counsel of the release of emotional stamina

Jesus lives because we are his abundant joyous blessing that calls you to pray

Heaven can be a place of a kind of joy we can never ever force on anyone

Truly distant relationships, can't be denied by the chances of everlasting delivery

Justice for the kind of differences we do not want to forget

The loyalty of family relationships is not domestic as the gentle breeze

Hindrance can jointly give the gentle justice for the indigent individual

The justice for the righteous is unbelievable

Trust that the universe is coming in your favor

I do not understand the cowardness of any individual

The collective animal is changing from the kingdom of reality of the kindness to the reality for the distance cannot come from the liberty of the reasonable kind Please rest assured the south is built on noncompliance of the captive audience Justification for a horrible experience can be limited to the counsel for the completion Science has evidence of such reasoning to the unkind person

Believe in who you can become on a daily basis for unselfish reasons

The light for completion is noncompliant with who you have become sensitive

Join us in allowing the coward persons to be enlightened with strength along with fortitude

Chancing human dignity and latent legacy of the kind of wisdom that would have been natural to me

Just relax and enjoy your gift provided to you by a legacy of human knowledge

I want the love and trust to be as natural as it would have been in person

I want to thank my natural ability stolen by an abusive animal trying to be a man but had no guidance

Justify

Behold now, I have ordered my cause; I know I shall be justified.

—Job 13:18

The remnants of satisfaction and the readiness associated with the guilty conscious of the rebuttal of suicidal reasoning of the likeness of resourceful feelings from the worldly desire to resee the threatened female who became a dork during the consequences of relatively kindness of falcons on a windy peak.

The closest setting for this redundant, sustained beginning of satisfied individuals who become lonesome in times of adverse sorrows and worrisome world refuses to expedite the process for a more hardy existence.

Cosmetic signs of cautious windless rhythms are questionable symptoms of grace and quest for a more greater existence of readiness by symbolic persons of personal gratitude and customs. Please reduce the latent candidacy of respirations during southern satire. The world is not ready to accept a change that has already happened

Heroines are not ignorant devices of old lectures from our latent reasoning from across the nation to be suitable for the reality of selfish patterns of luscious improper reasonable satire for the adult atmosphere.

The reason for this election can be seen through the important relief for selfish reasons.

Please remember, to live a life of reasonable constitutional universe, the enlightenment can be a religion for foreign affairs.

The case is illegal commentary for the gain of river scenic recluse associates is more than a reason to live in restoration and planning to begin the new life provided by the laws of the realist. Genius can be reemphasized according to the goals set by the individual who plans a life of stylish display.

Lower classes considered to be nonexistent in some market dynamics.

Chess games with strategies of winning the lottery and becoming a misinformed individuals.

We will, one day, be a very valuable asset to this country and the importance of emphasizing the word of joy and happiness and strength for the future.

Beauty is in the eye of the beholder. Do not forget cultural experiences are a category for the pleasantry of the last trust of individual hasting to fun times of the green deductions of character and profile satisfaction to be seen the false indignant resourceful neglect of the soul. Justification of a fake or innocent person and invasion of privacy that even the Lord our God cannot refute the expansion to be selected by restful exalt the vast majority of masses of people in the terrible campaign to clear their name although they participated in unbearable acts to be successful again in a timely nondedicated personable being although satanic practice was chanting for nonconformity of the majority seek revenue as an answer for going in the future. The detriment to be Armageddon soldiers of repost is thrown from wretched soldiers who were against being restored responsible adults. I remember the costly price of disloyalty by key players.

The psychotic, overpopulated societal remembrance of days of general insincerity of the people who did not properly care for the dominant child who sacrificed for a family secret was partially admired by community leadership.

The community could not forget my personal aspirations or dreams that I enclosed in projects that were personal reports for leaders of a world-class research guidance for the people who admired the dreams of one individual who educated the community about deficits that need to be addressed by community leadership advocate for a national organization goal planning.

To explain planning for the shortcomings of a community confidence and profile for future planning, leadership often admired individual accomplishments that went uncomfortable during times of being misinformed by reprehensible by lay leadership.

The timing is perfect due to impropriety of the person who cares for her.

She cannot even discuss the loyalty of the nonleadership associated with the medium walk of life

Just continue being a woman of character and faith for long, not strengthened for over thirty years of travesty.

The reticent coward has no consciousness to lead anyone to the darkest of time and never goes beyond the quality of miracle verses of dump in me musical interlude that will never receive the loving touch of Angels with all the trimming assets of worth outstanding for most mortals to be hold.

All I want is the opportunity to be in assistance in a powerful understanding that abounds for the multitudes.

Just the mechanism of truth for the underdog could understand the sound perfection that is needed in the industry.

Please place emphasize on life at the style of persons causing much trouble. What do you say after such a massacre?

The life of an individual is pertinent to sustain for others.

Pleasantries are only life masks for not being available to important parts in life.

We can't imagine what you went through as they attempted to make you conform to the South's traumatic and humiliating vestal deeds and random issues of the Western civilization. The citizens often reach the remnants of the ultimate recluse to be emulated.

The most convincing thing ever stated was, the power of costly reprisal is evidence of the concerned community members' readiness to accept the change of industry practices and business construction of the poetic reasoning shattered by constraints of the tempted imagination resulting in in compatible sensation.

Masses of citizens are concerned about the haphazard situations that are dehumanized with little meaning to aspire to improvement, and reasons for emptiness associated with loss and questionable circumstances revealed the justice and lofty goal set.

Reasonably, the aspects of the rightful concepts of genuine circumstances are not relevant to answer specific questions of the likely restful peace.

We are often reluctant to restore the climate to a place of institutionalized care of the restful potential for costly or vast likelihood of reservations that are literally explosive human dialogue associated with the least costly atmosphere that keeps the resistant to a fair minimum constitution.

The reason for disloyalty is not being able to reserve the willingness of the exterior to convincingly express themselves more for the good of the universe.

Quality individuals are like the crazed king who has just received the proper burial for the rights, literally seen circumstances along with the caliber of enhancing enthusiasm and conscious to relieve the mortal body to excuse of the nations.

Please encounter the wellness of lasting the victory of eternal reference to leadership.

The export of goods is guaranteed to be in the enlightened personal property to release your filtration of the heightened kindness.

Please remember the host of the temple to restore the evolution of restful toils.

Rightly gates are the reason for the massacre.

Royal qualities are the emblem for counsel of the franchise, fashionable cost of the random spacious mountain for the refusal of the stationary edification, and the cost of the successful refuge of the vast segregation of the policies of the national fruits from farmers and business practices of the ultimate allowances of the leadership chance for the lost express the reminders of the past results for service of individuals in the industry.

Please be a national resources for the religious irregularities.

Quick study for the complacent justice: We are not successful leaders.

The joy of the recent exposure of the weekly encounters of the restful justice seeking the counsel for the main gratifying gradual changes for the firmament viable as the loyalties for the quality individuals that are unkind forces to restress the guidance reference behind the remnants likely to be reprisal of the forgetful journey for the cowardly efforts that justify the refuge associated with the poetry of the children that are not zealous of the welcoming filament.

We suffer for the differences of the necessary frightened community restitution.

Counsel for the loyalties' differences was heightened for the reckoning of gentle citizens.

Lost chances are your misfortune needed for the utmost beacon of sentencing of the massacre.

Traumatic Southern ways of doing resting review.

The chastened mind justified for the cleansing of the mind.

Justice is rated in character living for the hindsight, reality for the conscious soul, restful united tragedy, and recluse for the language closest to the different allotments for the quickest vast network workable justice along with the rightly character and mature adults for the collegiate kind of limited recent solace guiding the light for the reticent language for the decent fracture look for the sacrifice of the reticent quality genius tragic likeliness doing the chastening foreclosure of meaningful costly consult for the soulful beneath the giant gentleness for the zealous temperament loss associated with the duty of friendly cues consenting the Gemini of fragrant fragrance.

The decision of the duty as the vast majority kill: We deliver the corpse for the gracious gravesite.

Salvatore Italian lineage to unite the United States mourning of mourners.

Justifiable faith associated with the commonwealth, the statue for sacrifice is still rewinding during times of impeachment. Society is seeking the type of mortal impropriety of the readers as the selfish, untiring efforts are related to the counsel of the caustic, rustic, the promise, sturdy reasoning, and the youthful daughter along with the ratings and differences stolen for the liquid channels of chance.

The lady saw the universal quality individuals.

Your citizens are a recluse for decades longer than usual.

Please release the rotary rotation in Texas.

The first good of champion statesman of the because of the restorative, years of abuse of the elderly in their homes.

Please financial backing offered for their crimes along with comedy.

We forget the justice in local towns and communities.

Please receive the challenges associated with the eyes of the sparrow.

Seeing the light of day.

The readiness of the supreme harvest associated with the displeasure of genius children is the welcoming person, readiness, and kindness that reap the contributions of the local police.

The clientele for the secondary reasonable licensed authority.

Quickly savage the retribution of the likely various systems.

Please send religious study of a solitude place.

The second licensed person sent to the less fortunate than self. Seniors are viable resource that settled down people who are also the alliances for the certainty. Please send favors of favorable expense.

The sailors seldom search the worthy lessons of the selfish sanctification.

The problem is the leadership of the others for the safety of liberation.

The ultimate sacrifice of the needy selfish likelihood of the sensible adult massacre.

The lesson is the mother of all rationality of change.

Massacre

And the spirit of the Lord came mightily upon him and he found a new jawbone of an ass and slew a thousand men therewith.

—Judges 15:14–15

Please take each day with enrichment if you enjoy each individual as an iconic authority that was created for a specific adventure.

The theme for this adventure is the Western World massacre that has caused anxiety as we travel down a rigorous path of adventures that can't be forgotten within any human's lifetime of justice recreation that would have solemnity as the government reassign the assassins of this massacre. Please have a sound existence that expects the universe to be related to the saints of a dying traumatic understanding of tireless universal sadness of the life that exists for the reading of the will. I hope one day to love again. Please request a reasonable folly for the life of the diseased mind.

One day, we will all discover the restful reliance we once had becomes redundant and peculiar to a personal relationship with the restful state of the land. I won't ever be a person who go against a person like you.

Please just provide the opportunity for the next meeting to be meaningful to others who suffered before the timing of relations.

Please accept the universal thought processes of coming to a transition of restful leadership of others who came before us.

Seeking the timely processes associated with the restful transient crises of current hope and graceful quietness of today's goodness culturally different than ourselves, yet we accept those differences with dignity and the grace of the Lord Jesus Christ.

Please consider the spacious ridiculous, restless jealousy and reluctant, resistant, and rough exterior of the sanctified recluse who reacted to the eclipse of raptured, tormented, invented endurance associated with illegal activity of the cancelled redundant required socialite of the indicative results and captive reason for not completing the versant campaign in the refusal of captive results that retrieved a lot of emptiness, associate with the physical changes that could result in direct resolution for actions not considered directly read a kind of rushed atmosphere that is common for aristocratic individuals in higher brackets of financial assets to be depleted and reserved for a party of living results that were recorded for the cancelling of campaign of justification for reliance of the vesting of reserved financial assets for humanity kindness. Adults do not reason for getting assets in traumatic crises of torment and dynamic value system for family.

I just want the energy of a resilient child who could be a dynamic person of residual chances for the season chances, who roughly reject the classic reliance on the other for charity chances for a successful adventures of happiness and refusal of change management, reluctant talents that are hidden from fortunate unconcerned captive futures of genuine results of regal majesty. I want to be beguiled and enchanted by fornication forbidden by the restless queenly estate. Rightly, tenacious gainful dilemma gaining teaguely farthest from the native Gemini attitude of graceful regard for the masses. Earth links along with the long surfaces to be explored more often than intended to be rustic gesture.

I vaguely return the favorable nest due to returns of remnants to be interchangeable with the community. The native would present their innermost meanings for a straightened attitude.

Willingly the community refused to comprehend the immortal totality assistance of foreign relatives.

Associates recanted some sexual defiance, resistance, and carbuncle references to unusual abnormal practices of innocence along with pressured elderly propensity for regurgitation of information to not appearing eccentric in any specific unnatural area associated with defiance against the opposite abnormal practices of these differences for the sake of restful sleep.

Please consider the foresight for which race, creed, and ambiguity have to trigger enormous enlightenment of seeds of compilation of necessary heartache, sincerity, and conditions of loneliness for millions and trillions of individuals across a nation of despair.

We must never forget the deeds of this life.

The Master is healer of all healers.

We do not have a chance without compliance.

We must persevere to select friends, confidants, close relations, and people of different nationalities.

I am appalled at the unkindness of choices they have made against humanity.

I shall, one day, look upon the faces of these individuals to become less than happy cousins in a world of unloyalty, kindness, forgery, kidnapping, sex, immorality, and ignorance.

Please forgive us, Master, for the living and the dead that we caused despair, mental enlightenment, and senseless murders within their hearts and flourishing immaturity of elderly individuals who can't control their faculties of immoral, lower-class attitudes but continue to act cowardly and childish from past experiences.

I believe individuals are becoming too unkind toward the love of others. We, as constant institutionalized people, can't possibly provide the knowledge based on lower-class structure that could happen to the world of infrastructure and leniency toward unkindness and misery on the present day.

Lord of host, please provide an anchor to be challenged and lead by a person of solitude and enrichment.

I want to forget the challenges or individuals who once believed in me as an individual.

Who once lived a life of happiness, contentment, graciousness, and
of helping mankind excel in their individual endeavors.
Please grant me grace, mercy, and liberation toward human kindness.
Please pray for those souls who couldn't adjust to these oppositions
that face our land.
As we close our hearts and souls to the man who made my life incom-
plete will, one day, secure my future life exhilarating and worthy
again.
I have many accomplishments that will be forgotten only to those
who did come into my present life but formerly came in the
next petition of greatness and learning externally to repose and
reposition me to a life of new attitudes for the future life for me
and my family.
In closing, I would like to express my gratitude toward a world that
will never know what I could have been and now will become.

Historical Recluse

Be still and know I am God.

—Psalm 46:10

Reference the giant of educational reduction.

The restrung vices are relenting for some. Seldom refreshed occurrences not held together by threadless, unchanging, relenting, cold remorse, religion, and uncaring ministerial revenue not received by congregational distance in a new century in an unchanging environment. I have resounded a society of religious unbelief and unbiased believers who attempt to escape the reality of the desolate, restful college of the dynamic history of the kind of souls to complain the science of conscience trials associated with the antics of religious compact readjustment of the ruin of chance reality.

We as crises of the dangers of recent ranges of reigning counsel.

The recent justice system has to be readjusting to godly stamina to convey resources of recent crimes associated with the silliness-refined reasons of a timetable readjustment.

I cannot imagine a generous obscenity of readjustment ascertain social goodness.

I reexamine readiness of change management.

Restful beginnings cannot convey opposite chances of winning.

Ordinarily, chances transcend enlightenment.

Readjustment of just caustic chances accessible to relying on a job chances often regains in recovery change.

Restful kindness revealed to candidates for vast reasoning to reverse the wrongs of the historian slave.

The descendants often have not seen or discovered the rules to make the right decisions, enlightenment, and recovery, along with chance resolutions.

The corners of my glorious reason for chancing. The limited situation of the cancerous consequences in the ground of religion.

We are justifiable in our actions. Please consider the restless causes of the entire entity. I ask for forgiveness associated with the kindness of loose motions associated with counsel and dying of the world kindness reviewed by public display, causing problems to bring negative feelings.

The cautious facet reasons for the rhythm of getting the significant changes to the reckoning of bullying can't stop sending signals of transformation of their existence to prepare the souls of godly persons to hypnotize the Spirit of the Lord.

Just listen at the leaves rustling and the restful peace of the lanterns that are sworn by recognition of gratitude and many blessings of grace, faithfulness, and constitutional rights of every individual to have a recovering mindset to believe in by grabbing the laws of the land.

Recently, I discovered the blooms on trees and the graceful look of the kind of significant person who is listening to make an extreme consonant restful and kind expression of gratitude and watchful grace from godly graciousness.

Not having enough energy to display naturally compromising subjects to relinquish the restful subjection for common ground of reasonable restitution, foreign policy, and troublesome guidance associated with justice, along with defiant, reckoning power through a population of recluse individuals, being put to use in the classes of race, creed, and living sacrifice for equal spacious climbing to a reckless power of missed confusion among tedious leaders in a restful steward to advancement around depletion to deploy a kind of circumstance of leading men among small rural townships that could not review the crisis-less appetite for the input of adverse circumstances that were useless for the creation of a defiant individual who made it a costly experience for gathering candidates for insignificant, unopposed right to hurt other resourceful people who have a spirit of sexual incontinence for being a selfish usage of financial reasons for subject dismissal.

The turning point came shortly after the sun diminished and after requests were made.

The gathering of light fixtures was the maintained warrior of the everlasting circle of other reasons of the listening audience.

The consequences to the latent party will always stop the fatigue of not going to the wretched cowardice quest for leniency against their wrongs.

The jasmine of sacrifice will, one day, release the table of contents for renewal against a custom magnitude of madness that overshadows the indignant preferences of living in a taunting cause for gentle relaxation, trust, enlightenment, individual accountability, ascension, and territory example of the present reliance of the reduction of the extreme interest belated individual hassle-free jealous contentions dispute from betraying regards for human life—the muscling of the human or humane disbelief of others.

The kind of reliance on others became restful and unenduring for selfish circumstances, caliber of lasting auditory restraint.

Best wavelength for assistance is justice for the most resiliency of the recluse despair. I want to be able to peacefully guarantee the listening to the loyalty of the participants associated with the candidacy of reasoning, filtering the combative, caustic resources. The results of the pillow talks are relevant for societal needs.

The residents involved are reluctant to provide this type of activity and should have the right not to do so.

The elderly should not be preyed by the public persona.

The counsel for the release of the target atmosphere for not being a part of the leadership of the ransom definite counsel of rejects is not loyal to anybody who did not seem to understand what actually matters and what doesn't.

Cautious announcements can be limited to the granted pregnancy of challenges associated with the elderly and the abusers.

The candidates for their legal obligations cannot resist for the reality of restless memories of the legal aspects of reasoning of the granted substitution, along with the leadership team approach for the candidacy associated with change.

The stupidity associated with that kind of activity can be unconstitutional and foreign to the beliefs of other people in the community test for incompetent behavior of the latter witnesses by their own wishful way of occurrences of the indifferent less rest physically and allow the world to be involved in the closure associates the attraction cases are reluctant to reside in the equal assistance and avenues for restoration and failure to document important belongings of the regents that once was petrified at the thought of ranking in the lower or upper regions in society to reveal an advance regular sensational formation associated during a time of inevitable reasoning the destiny of the rapture kindred gifts.

Wisdom endured exceptional rustic, autistic, persuasion, deception, remnants of devastation reliance of the leaders of mainstream acknowledgment. We are readjusted to emptiness of restoration that seems endless. The rental estate is rhetorical to renting a value system of challenges.

The worship of values is reluctant to unresourceful and recent distaining reduction of orient oligarchy.

Leaders can't be too public by an economic standards.

Please review candidates of every cultural discipline before becoming accepting of registrant and unloyalty, militant and redundant oligarchy

Reality has shown not so obsidian concentrate for the likelihood of becoming an obsolete being associated with an exterior that can be volcanic when it comes to discovery.

Location of this obligatory societal socialite, sustainable, culturally insignificant results of owner reliability associated with nonconformity of indignant and poignant exterior.

The residency of these individuals is rejection, control forces, and unseen challenges of square business.

Dynamics of a creditable audience, the lesson learned. The dynamic of the rest of reality of the nation

The kindness of the universe is a sign someone is unique the question is the place for complacency is not acceptable for the universe to believe.

I do not want to be unkind but release the deficit that comes with not loving a person as you should.

I do not want to be overlooked because of a kindler of not being the kind of person you think you should be.

The kindness should never had been listed the justice of another unkind individual that can never be tested.

Please consider the registration of the religion has been stopped due to not acknowledging a person of certain ethnicity or race. The release of such information is unreliable. Rethinking a relationship is sometimes spiritual.

The Master

A disciple is not above his teacher, but everyone
when he is fully trained will be like his teacher.

—Luke 6:40

Let's see the abuses from my eyes.

I do not like a person to be restless and unreliable to the restitution
associated along the paths of incongruent, inconvenient, selfish
concerns that do not belong in their rewarding deletion.

The list of living suspects is vicarious.

Pleasing resentment is going outside spears.

Restitution is all vehemently trying in venues of aging that are relent-
less in being prey to victimization.

The standard for abuse is not being responsible caretakers for an
elderly individual not provided with proper refuge for redun-
dancy associated with unkind individuals or relationships.

In the war associated with these types of individuals, please research
behaviors absent from the scene.

More than needed, the pain will be manifested in an unconditional
lawlessness-committed crime.

The tunic of destruction is the reputation of the assailants that are in
excusable for the world to reason.

The Master is the person that you feel is unsuspecting. That sort of
behavior constructs a timeless reputation that needs review.

At last, life returns to the what is personable. Look toward resources
that'll fall within reach of a damaged psychological solitude.

Children sometimes cannot fathom that youthful reason along the
recovery is reinstitutionalized.

The vacancy is refused by generations of living human beings.

The home of resident is not that reluctant to discuss the attire of reasonable demonstration of the relentless relationships, considered an anecdote, resident, and childish. References toward abusive language of the culprits of disloyalty, ransom, delicacies of inhumane flesh are their crimes.

Reasonable rental of reputable insufficient restless destiny.

The trenches is where they threw their victims.

The results were of disloyalties, restlessness, and indecency.

Rude behavior and wrenching nightmares by their victims caused insanity.

Protection often causes the insane immaturity, as the ruffled words, the revenue received from events, were reluctant to receive royalties.

This a ridiculous statue associated with the grandeur of abuse.

We are forever responsible as a nation for this national tragedy.

The nation should always seek restitution for a national tragedy.

Seek counsel from the Savior to be completely private.

We, as mankind, citizens should never risk a life for selfish, cruel gain.

Wretched individuals are dangerous and ignorant. Their poor genetic makeup is as if a serial killer was reaping habit on the helpless and destroyed on the geriatric community. Reluctance is among the world artifacts which of course are not needed.

Reiterate that the common man is not reputable to restrain from his selfish desires. Please refute any hostile behavior displayed to responsible, unreligious, negative, infiltering and lustful, passionate, unnatural respect for human suspects. Reality is not displayed or mastered.

On the recent unlikely display of recent recovery, all the distance and justifiable relations are disloyalty, resonance, despiteful discussions, and disgrace along the boredom assembled according to recent events of loyalty, rejection, and absentminded millennials showcasing stages of reliance on others for nontraditional responses.

Please review the kind reason for living in distant reluctant research of realist to examine the reduction of the role of joking relatively to mockery and tradition. We are in crises association of the reason.

I want to become something I just can't possibly be.

I just felt reduced to allowing my friend to be recessed to being a recourse of love in unnatural, untamed reason for unsustained value associated with this type of union is rejoiced, reduced, and recomposed which is the last reason for not attempting to resent the relations of rushing along the reality of the somber reticent awkwardness of love lost for my private life.

Life choices are returned to distant, crazy events, relinquishing the years ahead and left behind.

Roasting a soulful cause, I hesitate for renown or restless confusion of individual choices of caution.

The enlightenment of sacrifice can be because no one is available to carry design and science, roasting an assassin, and restful plea for fruit that is forbidden.

I cannot rejoice in song or peaceful justifiable recourse for genius reward that is not available to novelty.

Lost but found without a proper, responsible loyalty of the opposite attraction of fools who just reasonably call their way of casualties that cannot change.

The husband and wife will always have challenges of distasteful, menial stupors that will just never receive.

I love the awkward teasing of unfamiliar territory.

The totality of this energetic response for living in a warrior statue.

Familiarity versus the reasonable torch of kindness reduced to restorative ignorance about the human dialect.

Roarful, indignant unpleasantness associated with unwarranted, unwanted abuse for choices.

Reasonably restful rejection can be inherited from formerly known relations with primarily the matriarch of societal reasons for the claim that could not be warranted.

Candidly, barriers become totality of genius counsel.

Let's forget the justifiable past cautions or cautions of the latest renal reject.

David was a man who was prideful and under pressures from the most powerful mediator in the earthly realm.

Tyranny is a point of no justifiable resident that is reasonably afraid of nature.

How do we carry out this rhetorical nature with a name of Jesus being a part of lives.

Destiny can be hidden in places of constant rejoiceful unhappiness.

I can't imagine a life rejoined without considering the unknown caustic, untalked-of discoveries.

Reasoning is irrefutable. The justifiable giant of the century is a discussion of chance.

Listening at lightning striking is not plausible or reckoning of circumstances.

Rejection often labels me as a trustworthy individual who relies on fortune or fame.

How can a harasser perceive you as a targeted individual who is not forgiven.

Restitute, restore, affiliate, and infiltrate the guidance of enlightenment restored.

We are reasoned for just thinking about kindness, restitution, consequences, and loyalty to mankind.

Reasoning can request an attitude of common results.

I do not understand relations of gratitude associated with rejected obsolete resistant confidence in a world transgressing into ransomed, unkind unknowns of resident respect and responsible payments for tangents.

Rest a loosen bow and forgo a reward of satanic resolutions for the unfortunate, destitute, justifiable political boundaries of soulful, wasteless regents or rehearsed coughing of classic clowns of the highest degree.

Lessons of gesture along with dynamic, classical resentment.

Restless partners are unjoyful, daunting rehearsal for rude and unrelaxed confidence in another person of sonnet forgetfulness.

The twelfth hour is journey in a warm loving atmosphere of relaxed reform.

Last citizen reacts to defenseless wrongs and claims a home for years before repurchasing the rights to gladiator moments.

I love the wealth and the resilience of low rescission associated with the collegiate arena.

The random chance of the Amsterdam resources is delectable, uncharted, and lonesome plane.

The rescinded, wretched, forgetful moment can be a barrier of discrimination of light-skinned persons of different origin than myself.

Reduction and laziness constitute radiance along with justifiable outings associated with running to oblivious condemnation.

Rushing to the caution of likeliness transcends outlandish familiar passages that cannot be a part of the world training room for the trendy session of the legal system to relish the opportunities to welcome the pleasant rushmead so sordid and content of the humane trials of the destiny of revisiting the insanely unretired listings of personal gratitude associates that are reluctant to visit with the person who reads a caliber of reasonable junction unity and burning undesirables.

The gatherings were quick assessments for the formidable review for obsolete occurrences that are not weathered with the assistance of membership.

Justice is a realm statue of associates and boss review to make future ramparts less cumbersome.

I really became reasonably uncomforted with the relations of the kind of affairs that needed to be compromised by blatant insecurity among membership.

The wrath of steadfast disloyal members would compromise negotiations.

The standard is the trust of each individual for team player to be an example of individual sanity for tasks to operate without a chance for greed, uncomfortable viable leadership strategy reluctance, guidance resolution, and negotiations.

Realist players are reasonably stylish and refuse to complete operations as previously planned in conjunction with the needs of organization structural control by insignificant dynamics not encouraged by the organization assessment of happenings.

Reorganization is susceptible for ranges of guest to input the ionic rejects who could not ascertain the thoughtless, unwarranted dialogue from the bosses' random assessment of events that happened previously by suspects who destroyed the team concept to rejoice the readiness of the group.

Review the Cavanaugh of vital curfew.

The latest confident group threats can be rehearsed by alliances outside the corners.

When favors are not returned to the original owners, then shortcuts can reduce the enterprise efforts to ascertain reasonable constituents for the type of rehearsed groups do not refuse one another's authority over territorial avenues, which would endanger a section that was bothersome to other radical organization structure, but respected against a rival who just realized its own individual power.

The consequences can jeopardize operations regarding change management.

Justice is not a target for the streets, just resolutions to be exposed or expected to take place in relation to nontraditional areas for some.

Juniors who are easily frightened are disbarred from being a participant.

Let's remember the local authorities that are often involved during proceedings which are unconstitutional to races of people who are unsuspecting of these surroundings.

Reversal proceedings will never be accepted or warranted by unsuspecting persons of undeniable, refutable, lasting return for the lone suspect.

Redemption or revisiting the seen character will be denied by the masses.

The reasoning is not sufficient for not trying to refute for concentrating on insufficient, restful allowances to consider the satanic sacrifice of the bullying sources who are only identified by prison public sanctification.

The authorities are unsuspecting of these devices surrounding them.

The victim is lessened by the ageless population.

The victims are changing from children to the elderly population.

Elders are just as susceptible to advances.

The restless giants can cartoon the elderly populations for trial on this population of unsuspecting rantings by the young unsuspecting public citizens.

The elderly are frail and have difficulty with explanations of experiences compared to children who are alert and witty, not randomly changing topics for formal witnesses.

The elderly conform out of fear of reproach by friends who judge their activity.

Friends become less due to peculiarity of actions observed.

The elderly become withdrawn due to fear of death by strong healthy individuals who threaten to uphold threats if they are not tolerated by their activity.

Warnings are upheld by injectable medical reasons that are brought in off the street camp by their abusers.

The elderly attacks are increasing as we are living longer.

Please beware of an aging population at risk and unsuspecting of their complicated future dealings with the young population.

Freedom is becoming a moral insanity for the young to control future infringement on public crimes to reduce law enforcement interference.

Readiness by the public is unsuspecting of this changing challenging way to corruption unnoticed by today's outdated management of community criminal crimes.

The City of Angelic Euphoria

But ye are a chosen generation, a royal priesthood, an holy nation,
a peculiar people; that ye should shew forth the praises of him
who hath called you out of darkness into a marvelous light.

—1 Peter 2:9

The sea upon ballistic embellishment, heartening sensitivity, the life
restless common practice, that supersedes talent infrequent to
hostility
The island of sacrifice is relentless
Please assist when gullible persons or individuals, are kind solace to a
distant relief of obvious, careless, childlike relevance
I have inspired artistic relations to growth, instant successful beings
I have foreseen enlightenment, relations, character, tainted, twisted,
untraditional, resolutionist,
rejection, heartless, unsophisticated attitudes, independent, unsup-
ported, and cowardly sources
Please consider obligations others could possibly joined without
justice
The attitudes associated currently are unreliable, uncaring, tragic,
unwilling, dumb cases of reliance of frugal, unpleasant, child-
less human beings of merciless trauma
I cannot receive such foolishness, unkindness, rejoice, helpless, hurt-
ful, resourcefulness, rejected souls
The proper approach would be candid, insignificant
Trials are a constant in outlandish memory, unsecure, unspoken,
ridiculous, pessimistic, and resurgence

I can't receive, life experiences are so reluctant, that people wouldn't consciously, go relentlessly, after a person privacy and rejoice at such sadness and enjoy doing a deed so hopeless

I want to rejoice in such unrenowned unclear responsible radiance

We will justify such unreliable consequences to the depth of jovial hassling of bigotry

Please reject the infamous mixture of listening to a practice of evilness by loyalist to their own default

The characteristic lewdness associates arrangements are inhumane I really have the courageous receptive universal phenomenon

Justice for certainty is historical, realist, unguarded, along the happenings to inspire restitution

Loyalist tried to ridicule the obvious correction of righteousness

The ceiling has a history emblem of graces that resemble a prenup agreement

Witnesses to a tyrant, tyranny, lonesome evidence refused by localist

The gathering of nontraditionalists can betray a confidence in a program of hurt, resistance, shame, adulterous, refute, due to mentality

Rest the lantern of shipmates associated with individuals rolling instantaneous rapture for selfish reasons that have no altitude for being unreliable, accusatory, bloodshed

The historical restitution, restraints, the restful, torture associated with silence, due to the mental capacity of the victims' ability to reason

In-depth mysteries of actual accounts of what happened are buried within the victims' soul

Discussions are oblivious to any of the victims' surroundings

The elderly are reduced to accepting the unreasonable circumstances associated with the decline in physical health

Our souls subconsciously alter the mindset

Rejoice with the Lord in cowardice situations that wouldn't be receptive to discuss

The world is reluctantly attempting to revive a generation divided by destruction, human error, class, race, and creed

One day the lessons will be highlights to successful citizens

The living relatives are distant, unsuccessful, not a part of your life

People now live alternative lifestyles that are redundant, rude, boastful, and not allowed to be near your children

The rhetorical highlights are going to be relieved of sarcasm, fault, along the road to recovery

Please understand that a personal contact will once be a gratitude of hope or selfishness

Relationships are insignificant to an alliance of fortitude, consequences, rather terrifying to rectify a lending, joyful solutions and invaluable risks in an individual's psyche

Convincing restless nonconcentrating victims to be harmed due to unrelenting results found prior to demise

Recent events are readily weird or unrelated to what is currently an unjustified incident that happened much earlier

Neither culprit is willing to sacrifice their life for admittance

The rejection by higher authorities will soon leave people unreliable and selfishness

Rejoice at what you were able to do out of awareness, unjustified leadership as a family

The person in charge is always the person who is most ridiculed by public demands

Projects like these are never renowned for the selective style by any persons

Recourse is nonevidence of sacrifices, unjustifiable by public exposure

Luckily the restoration is a difficult demand for years of exposure to harmful, untrusting people, who claim to never do any harm publicly hidden from societal pressures in seclusion from their crimes

Elderly victims and children become primary targets and cartilage for rapists; random, unreliable certainty; and radical inhumane conditions

The realist in me relates to relatively repetitious along the refusal of a person's timetable

The kind of specific clarity or clarification as it relates to unequal, unrelenting artifacts associated with the chase

I want to one day chance a consequence of schooling that was once considered dynamic registered right way, to approach anyone's reputation for being abusive to others

Let's remember places associated with this type of abuse

I cannot imagine a jerk, as wild or uncanny as retold a readily household

I also have not done similar, but understand, retold embellishment by others

Rejection is a ridiculous consequence for a person to have to endure

I want ever distress, the unprideful, relations that people have to endure as they age

Please consider recurrence of the anxious nature

Joining in a table of sacrifice, as it relates to relations or relatively routine

I have adorned myself with the consequences

The costs associated with this rejection and deed are asked to build on what I started

We have never received a personal fault of any kind resource or compliance

Relentless rejection should make the suspect feel awful or awkward in the individual's presence

I refuse to allow people to be mistreated in ways unknown to circumstances

I did not notice the disloyalty of people in positions of authority

Please place a statue of loyalty, lesson hostility associated with inhumane individuals

The reasoning of the recovery forces, associated with the most annihilate

The restoration with the running to the present junction

The revenue has returned to the relaxed courage associated with kindness

The reassurance of the grace of the cost waste of gesture

The lament trade assets the human form to be pleasing to the infamous trademark, to lesson is frightening

The story continues to involve whispers of tragedy that compromise the very outlook associated with the wise person of gentle, loving nature and natural political ecstasy, love channels and restive, likely uncommon encouragement

The last person to envision a relative person in collegiate atmospheric setting to settle in a position not related to constant change

Resting in an environment to list a revealing example of the common refusal for changing the recent forecast of unforeseen changes associated with the kind of reluctance of registration for membership causes

The lesson cannot stop being uneven for the legacy of resting to see a coward existence for religion basement of courage changes with moral character in a century of listless people in the company of locksmiths of forever stories of abridgment for clockwise company of parishioners to hope for morally correct individuals, who cannot express sensitive cooperative lessons learned

Justification of antics not welcomed by present-day common persons or people

Maturity is of most importance by challenging the status quo

Jewels are common practical gifts provided by the witnesses

Clean excitement is restless jump rope training constituents for change from one

Religious strike backs by masters reason for doing envious satisfaction of the fans who cleared

the way for civil changes around the continent resting on renown capture for a life never

restored for reasons of insecurity, loose luck not planned for the futuristic laziness of innocent,

infrequent juiceful competition of reluctance and inhousable jubilant and recent encounters

Rental plans are unreliable to all personnel excuses of regret for loosely grandeur environment

Control is reluctant for misery, love, company, and unsuspecting needs

Please consider the privacy for the sake of not knowing the legacy of the tradition of change I do not understand the likely control of the sense of style for the cleaning of the source that came and died for the memory of the legacy of style associated with the sensing of cultural office of southern style for the future of legacy of the long road for the results of local registration I do not want to send the ground of sources seen

Locally the rest of the jungle can reserve the right to send a resource to the legacy seen by the common man

You men make things difficult to analyze for product retail to reveal a common gracious clarity and understanding

Patience with God

I waited patiently for the Lord; he turned
to me and he heard my cry.

—Psalm 40:1

Please continue your journey toward greatness and sincerity
The journey became cumbersome, awful, and discouraging, unpleasant, useless, confusing, restricting, and earnestly not available for retribution

Let's begin a new start with a useful relentless, unbothered, and relaxing contribution to societal standards
Please come to a life of peaking before the mountain of celestial journey
Please just give the very thing God loves most is you
I am able to be a form of discipline that will not stop the timeless peace and living for some pleasing time as coming to a journey
I want life that builds on Christian values, faith, and justice
I have seen so many unlikely contributions to societal useless success for individuals who could care less about the journey that pleases persons of character and restraining
I can't possibly steal unpleasant moments that continue to be unkind
The lifeless position is unconditional for most persons, who like liberation or extreme circumstances associated with being a martyr
We need kindness, solace, reasoning suggestive resolution, kindness, just consider the fowls of the air
The fowls of the air contradict our custom's resolutionary convenience for each of us Please consider obligations of persons who

are less fortunate than yourself I am but a friend in waiting of every kind of blessing the world has provided I do not care if mankind will stop being socially incorrect unless persons of different races are taken into account the belief system of other familial relationships that are unkind, unreasonable, selfish, but personal to our unreasonable, selfish, but personal to our public display of relations of former friends, who once graced our presence to be unreliable, uncordial, relentless, greedy, but contrary to our consciousness

I always was the type to not criticize worldly events, that can't be dominated by persons not familiar with incidents flawless, unexpected, beneath psyche of our souls I can't acknowledge acts of turpitude, wisdom doesn't allow these unpopular creative thought in-depth, retrieval

I want to reverse common practice systems and to extinguish the torment associated with similar will

Please recognize unworthy individuals in the world who have considered interment

To acknowledge the life that comes out after demise is reluctance, gratitude but forgiving is utmost importance

Sometimes living life can be turmoil for a victim of abuse that we can't fathom being more than what was learned at an infallible age

I want to thank everyone who gives kindness understanding along with God's grace I am pleased that persons who have done awful unkind things during a process that has been years in the making

I have seen so many things that I don't want to ever have flaws that have been unkind to others

If I can one day see a land of kindness toward one another

We as a country will one day see a land free of the home and love kindness more than we love hate

Please consider the hope we have in Christ that has always come part of a long past differences of racial equality I don't understand the free press of today

We are a people who will not ever believe in the country of kindness
toward others

Please be sensitive to other's feelings and have a sincere heart that will
never be a part of this family

I want to admit to a life struggle that was a loose cannon Please con-
sider a kindness that will last for generations to come

I will not come to unkindness to be included with a crowd that will
not have conclusive language

Please consider dusk till dawn patience with all of life's changes do
not forget whose you are and enjoy a life of servitude and solace

Lifesaving Grace in Jesus's Name

For by grace you have been saved through faith; and
that not of yourselves, it is the gift of God.

—Ephesians 2:8

The sun always shines in heaven
It only shines when you make clarity of who you would become
Sometimes the noonday crises of daily living will always be a good
　　place to seek heaven's gateway
We soon forget the tidal wave that caused the massacre
Let's always remember that we can make dominions of lessons
　　throughout life, but the consequences of these are almost
　　nonexistent
Soon we forget what caused our massacre with life moving on in spite
　　of circumstances
The world is constantly moving in a direction of belief and draw-
　　backs I can't fathom the mysteries of the latest review, but citi-
　　zens of the universe are constantly reposing the spectrum
I want to forget mankind is a lot like being a symbol or collections of
　　events that often are reversed

About the Author

Rhonda Taliaferro Jones, MBA, grew up in a small rural county in West Tennessee (Brownsville).

Rhonda was an outstanding, applicable student of community outreach education, doing her tenure as a social worker in a number of outreach agencies including the American Cancer Society and Wo/Men's Resource and Rape Assistance Program. Rhonda's later career included being an instructor and academic adviser at her alma mater—University of Tennessee at Martin. She is also a graduate of Regis University, Denver, Colorado, with a master of business administration.

Rhonda "J" Taliaferro has been a native of Haywood County but resides in the city of Jackson, Tennessee. The most important or impressive duty she had in her life was when she was an instructor and adviser at the University of Tennessee at Martin, where she received her bachelor of science in psychology. Rhonda later received her Master of Business Administration from Regis University.

Rhonda also attended the University of Memphis, where she began to study for her doctorate in curriculum and education. Rhonda continues to seek education as a primary professional learner.

CPSIA information can be obtained
at www.ICGtesting.com
Printed in the USA
LVHW010014120422
715960LV00001B/123